1389

THE PEMBROKE
AND
TENBY RAILWAY

D1740761

by
M. R. C. Price

THE OAKWOOD PRESS

ISBN 0 85361 327 3

Printed and bound by S&S Press, Abingdon, Oxford

Bibliography

The Story of Pembroke Dock *by E.E. Peters.*
Top Sawyer (biography of D. Davies) *by I. Thomas.*
History of the Great Western Railway *by E.T. Macdermot.*
The Pembroke and Tenby Railway *by J.P. Morris.*
Railway Magazine *Volume 2, 1898, Page 560 by B.H. Thomas.*
The Locomotive, *15 August, 1912, Page 164 by Sir O.H.P. Scourfield.*
Railway Magazine *Volume 35, 1914, Page 65, 139 by G.W.J. Potter.*
Railway Magazine *Volume 105, 1959, Page 663 by H.A. Vallance.*

Acknowledgements

The Public Record Office (British Transport Archives); The House of Lords Record Office; The National Library of Wales, Aberystwyth; Pembrokeshire County Record Office, Haverfordwest; Pembrokeshire County Library, Haverfordwest; Cambridge University Library; The Mitchell Library, Glasgow; Manchester Central Library; Chesterfield Central Library; British Railways (W.R.), Cardiff; Tenby Museum; The Historical Model Railway Society; The Branch Line Society; The Great Western Society; *The Western Telegraph,* Haverfordwest.

R.E. Bowen, M. Brace, H.C. Casserley, T. David, F.K. Davies, G.J. Davies, R. Daniells, G. Dow, N. Edwards, J.W. Evans, J.J. Francis, D.G. Geldard, W. Griffiths, G. Harris, W. Harrison, J.S. Holden, R. Howells, H.G. James, S.C. Jenkins, R.A. Kennedy, the late E.T. Lewis, E.R. Mountford, Rev. W.R. Nicholas, J.K. Reed, Mrs E. Skone, J.N. Slinn, Mr & Mrs J. Stredder, W.C. Thombs, E.S. Tonks, E. Williams, R. Worsley.

Published by
The OAKWOOD PRESS
P.O.Box 122, Headington, Oxford.

THE PEMBROKE AND TENBY RAILWAY

Contents

Introduction

For a thousand years the old county of Pembrokeshire was distinguished by an unseen frontier — the Landsker — separating the north from the south. The Landsker was (and still is) primarily a language and social division, between the Welsh speaking north and the English speaking south. However, it has often been noted that this frontier is also marked by boundaries of geology and landscape, the wilder uplands of the Prescellys being in complete contrast to the gentler rural landscape of the south, the "Little England beyond Wales" of imposing Norman castles, castellated church towers and Anglo-Saxon place names.

In railway terms, the Landsker may be said to approximate to the position of Pembrokeshire's first portion of main line, opened between Whitland and Haverfordwest in January, 1854. The branches built later to the north — to Cardigan and to Maenclochog — were as Welsh in character as anywhere in the entire Principality. The long branch to the south, the Pembroke & Tenby, was much more English — and arguably made so in part by the experience of military traffic. An inspector who once visited the Cardigan and the Pembroke lines in the same week declared that the distinction was quite evident: if he opened a desk or drawer at a station or signal box going north he would find chapel papers, probably in Welsh. Going south he would find a copy of the racing news!

It is about a quarter of a century since my first journey over the P&T, at a time when Great Western steam was still supreme, the busy little stations were still staffed, and the summer Saturday traffic at Tenby was a pleasure to see. The "Pembroke Coast Express" then provided the highlight of the day, headed by a gleaming green engine — maybe a "Manor" 4–6–0 or a "Mogul" or sometimes a "Prairie" tank. Now the barking, copper capped engines and the through coaches to Paddington have gone, but at least the P&T line itself is still with us. If you know it, this history may add to your interest. If you don't know it, maybe this account will encourage you to travel the line for yourself, and so help to keep it in business. At all events, I must express my grateful thanks to many people who have helped me in my study. As the manuscript in its original form was completed in 1978, I must also thank them for their patience! Special mention must be made of my wife, Judy, for all her support over the years, and particular thanks are due to Ray Bowen for his encouragement and wise counsel at various stages of the study. My thanks, too, to G.J. Davies, who very kindly allowed me to see the fruit of his work on the subject. Further acknowledgements are given at the end.

Martin R. Connop Price.
Hook Norton, Oxfordshire.
September, 1986.

Chapter One
The Route Described

South Pembrokeshire is an area of remarkable natural beauty, quiet undulating farmland meeting the sea in rocky coves, high cliffs and unspoilt sandy beaches. Inland the eastern and western arms of the Cleddau river meet in the sheltered deep water harbour of Milford Haven, recognised for centuries as one of the finest natural harbours in Britain. In spite of its remote situation, Milford Haven had obvious potential in the nineteenth century for those anxious to develop commercial links with Ireland and America. Today, although the first railway terminus on the Haven — at Neyland — has closed, two lines still approach its shores. One route runs to the town of Milford Haven on the north shore, and now derives much of its traffic from nearby oil refineries. The other line runs to Pembroke Dock on the southern shore, by way of the holiday resort of Tenby. This is the line which began life as the Pembroke & Tenby Railway.

The junction between the main line to Milford Haven and the branch to Pembroke Dock is at Whitland, in what was Carmarthenshire. Whitland Station is 233¾ miles from Paddington via the Severn Tunnel, but the mileposts measure by the original route via Gloucester, and make the distance 259 miles. Nowadays the station has two through platforms on the main line, and a bay platform on the down side for Pembroke Dock trains not travelling on to Carmarthen or Swansea. Probably few passengers for the branch give more than a glance to the nearby site of the locomotive shed and the P&TR's own station, now cleared and partly in commercial use. The branch becomes a single track almost as soon as it leaves the main line at the west end of Whitland station. It then climbs through pleasant open country on gradually steepening gradients towards Narberth, five miles distant in Pembrokeshire. Narberth station is approached on a gradient of 1 in 50 for about a mile, and here, although the platform on the up side is the only one in use, its P&T station building still stands in 1985. The old goods shed also survives, although the goods yard is no longer railway property.

Beyond the station the line rises on a 1 in 85 gradient, and enters the 273 yard Narberth tunnel. In the steam era this could present drivers with a real challenge, especially on wet days. Furthermore, as the tunnel is on a tight curve it is very dark: permanent way men have often guided themselves through by tapping along the rails with sticks!

The track continues to climb until Cold Blow summit is reached in a rather desolate area almost two miles beyond Narberth. The descent from this aptly-named spot is as rapid as the climb, the gradients

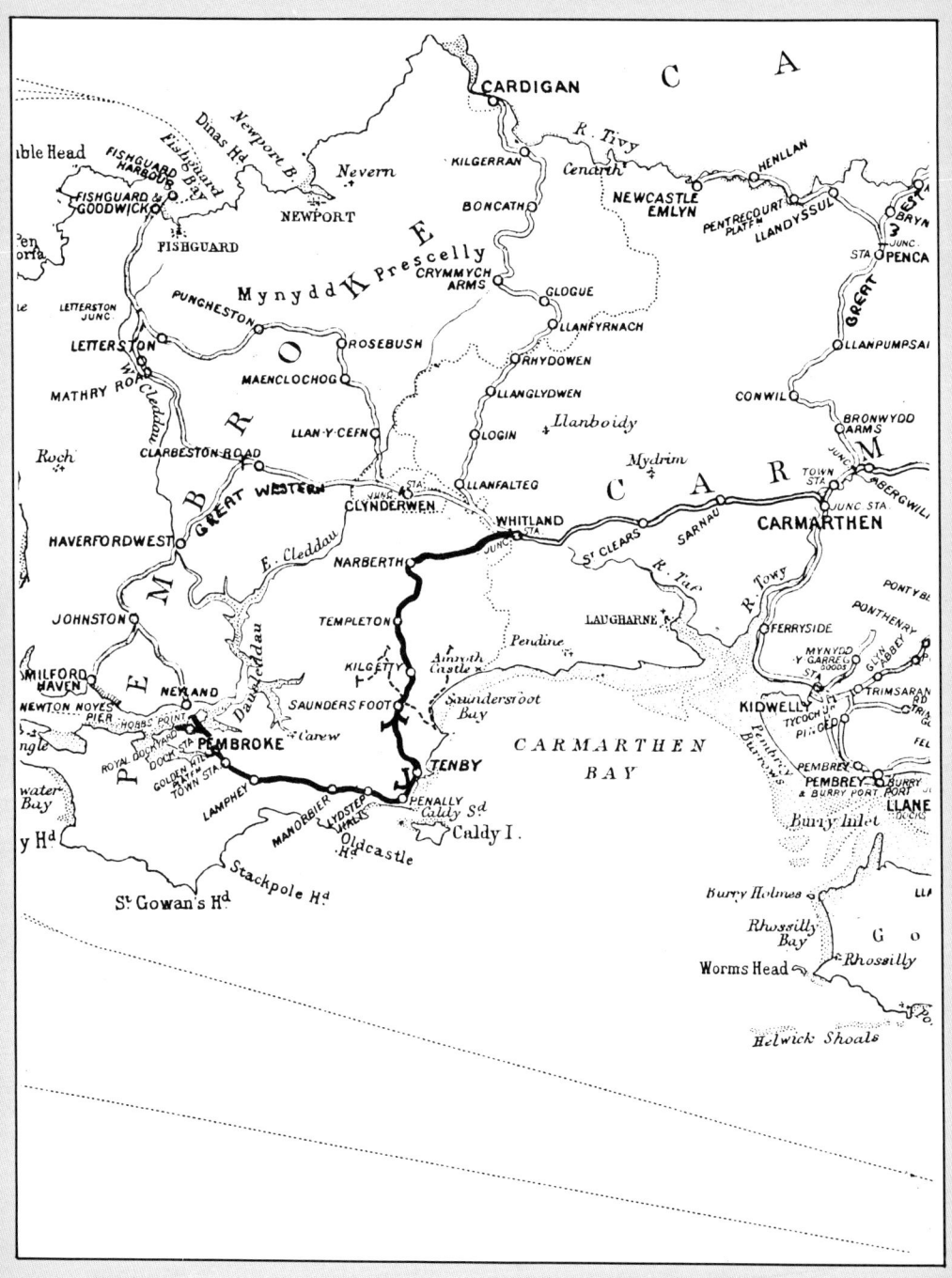

falling at up to 1 in 47 over the next one and a half miles to Templeton. Here the site of the closed station is marked merely by two deserted platforms, and bushes grow where sidings twice stabled the Royal train.

South of Templeton the railway continues on undulating and much easier gradients to Kilgetty (10¼ miles), a station originally known as Kilgetty & Begelly, as the latter village is so close as to be in sight. Today the station's single platform supports no more than a shed and a concrete waiting shelter, and the former goods yard is occupied by coal merchants. After crossing the new Kilgetty by-pass the line reaches Saundersfoot (11 miles) where another concrete shelter is provided on the down platform, and both the up platform and the goods yard are derelict. At this point the railway crosses the long abandoned Pembrokeshire coalfield, but now there is little to be seen, south of Saundersfoot, of the site of sidings to the old collieries at Bonvilles Court and Moreton. It is rather easier to get a glimpse of the sea, scarcely a mile away to the east.

The railway descends towards Tenby on gradients as severe as 1 in 50, and approaches the station over a seven arch viaduct made of local limestone. Tenby (15¾ miles from Whitland) presents the most cheerful picture to be seen anywhere along the line. The station is staffed, buildings on both platforms are well maintained, and the presence of signals and a signal box lend an air of purpose to the scene. The goods shed and yard are now in the hands of builders merchants. The nearby Tenby Lower Yard has been cleared of railway buildings, and the site is occupied by a large car park.

Leaving Tenby the line runs behind sand dunes and a golf course to Penally. Half a mile south of Tenby a small stone hut on the west of the line marks the location of Black Rock junction. Nowadays it is hard to believe it ever was a junction: the route to the Lower Yard is overgrown, and the course of the old quarry siding is covered by a huge caravan park. Penally station (17 miles) retains a platform which is well used in the summer months, but the old station building is privately owned. Views of Caldy Island are now left behind as the line turns west and climbs at 1 in 75 and 1 in 83 towards the grassy platform at Lydstep. The next station is Manorbier (20 miles). Here, in the absence of station staff, the level crossing gates are opened and closed by train guards. Although the signal box and passing loop have been removed, fixed distant signals remain to give warning of the crossing. The station house is now in private hands.

The line is now on the edge of military Pembrokeshire — a glorious stretch of open country around Penally, Manorbier and Pembroke marked throughout this century by camps and troop training grounds. Beyond Manorbier Newton crossing, and the site of Beavers

Hill Halt, the railway reaches Lamphey (23½ miles). Always a somewhat undistinguished station, it now offers no more than a concrete
shelter for the comfort of passengers. The facilities at Pembroke (25
miles) are no better, although the presence of three sidings on the up
side misleadingly make it appear more business-like. The gaunt walls
of Pembroke Castle provide a reminder of tension in an earlier age as
the railway turns north-west and climbs at 1 in 59 to Golden Hill. The
halt has long gone, but the 460 yard tunnel still has a portal marked
"P. & T.R. 1863". Beyond, at Llanion crossing, a ground frame
controls access to Pembroke Dock goods yard, but the short branch to
Hobbs Point has been lifted. After passing the cleared site of the small
locomotive shed, the railway reaches Pembroke Dock station, refurbished in 1979/80. Although tracks remain at both platforms, only the
southern platform sees regular use. The long derelict extension to the
dockyard has been dismantled. In its restored condition the main
station building at Pembroke Dock provides a tangible reminder of
the P&TR and a fitting terminus for a journey which in steam days
was as rich in sounds as in sights, and which, even in the diesel era,
leaves a lasting mark on the memory.

PEMBROKE AND TENBY RAILWAY.

UP TRAINS—WEEK DAYS.

FROM	1 1, 2, gov.	2 1, 2.	3 1, 2.	4 1, 2, g.
	a.m.	a.m.	p.m.	p.m.
Tenby ... ... dep	7 30	......	1 0	5 15
Penally...	7 33	......	1 3	5 18
Manorbeer — St. Florence	7 41	......	1 14	5 29
Lamphey	7 50	......	1 25	5 40
Pembroke	7 55	...	1 30	5 45
Hobb's Point (coach) ...	8 30	.....	2 15	6 25
New Milford (ferry)	8 40	......	...	6 40

DOWN TRAINS—WEEK DAYS.

	a.m.	a.m.	p.m.	p.m.
Hobb's Point (ferry) ...	8 55	.....	2 30	6 43
Pembroke (coach) ...arr.	9 41	...	3 0	7 15

FROM	1, 2, gov.	1, 2	1, 2.	1, 2, gov.
Pembroke ... ... dep	10 0	......	3 15	7 30
Lamphey	10 5	......	3 20	7 35
Manorbeer—St. Florence ..	10 16	......	3 31	7 46
Penally...	10 27	......	3 42	7 57
Tenby	10 30	......	3 45	8 0

Timetable for December 1863.   *Courtesy Pembroke Record Office*

The next few pages show the track plans of stations down the line.

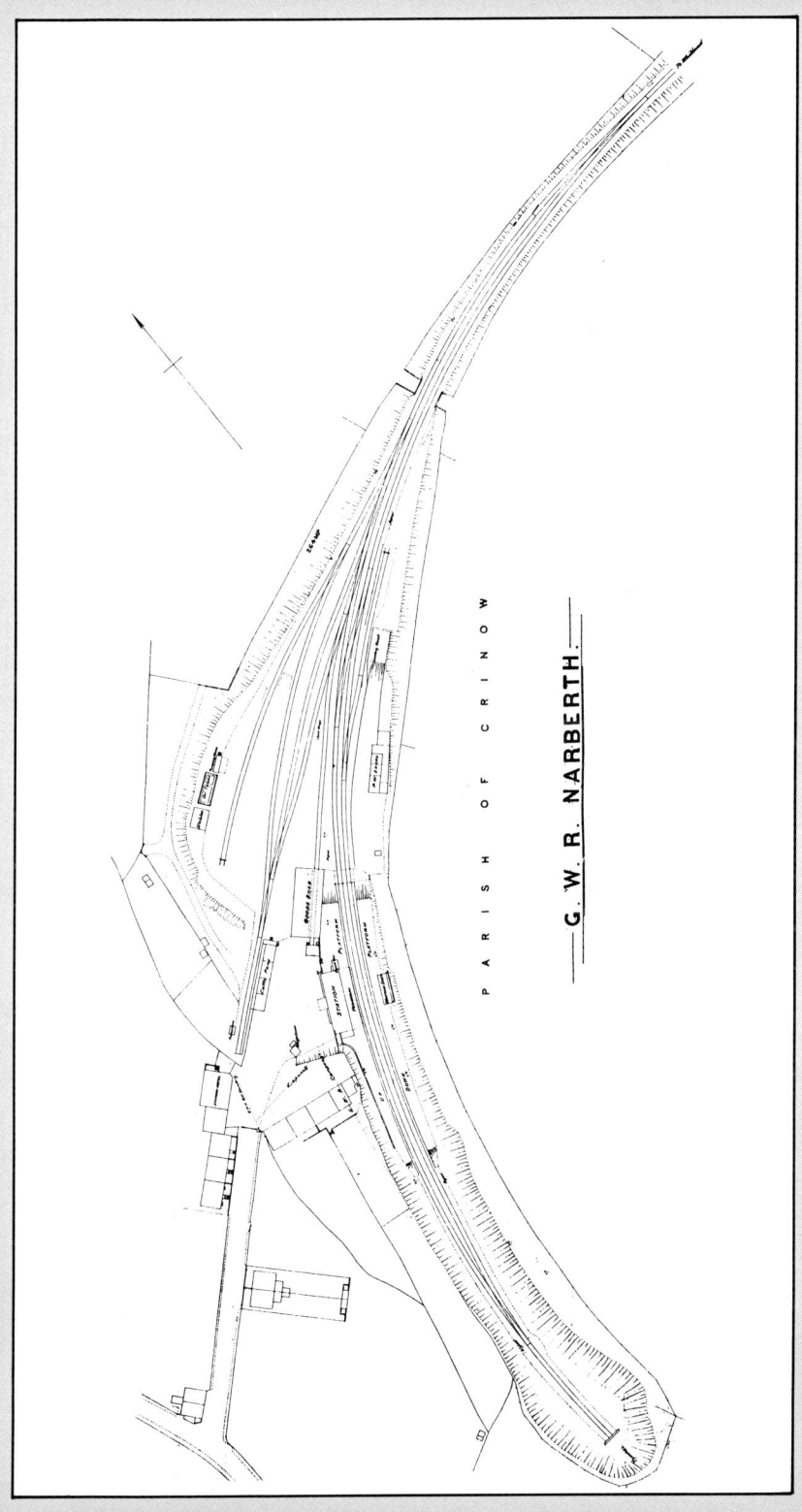

PARISH OF CRINOW

G. W. R. NARBERTH.

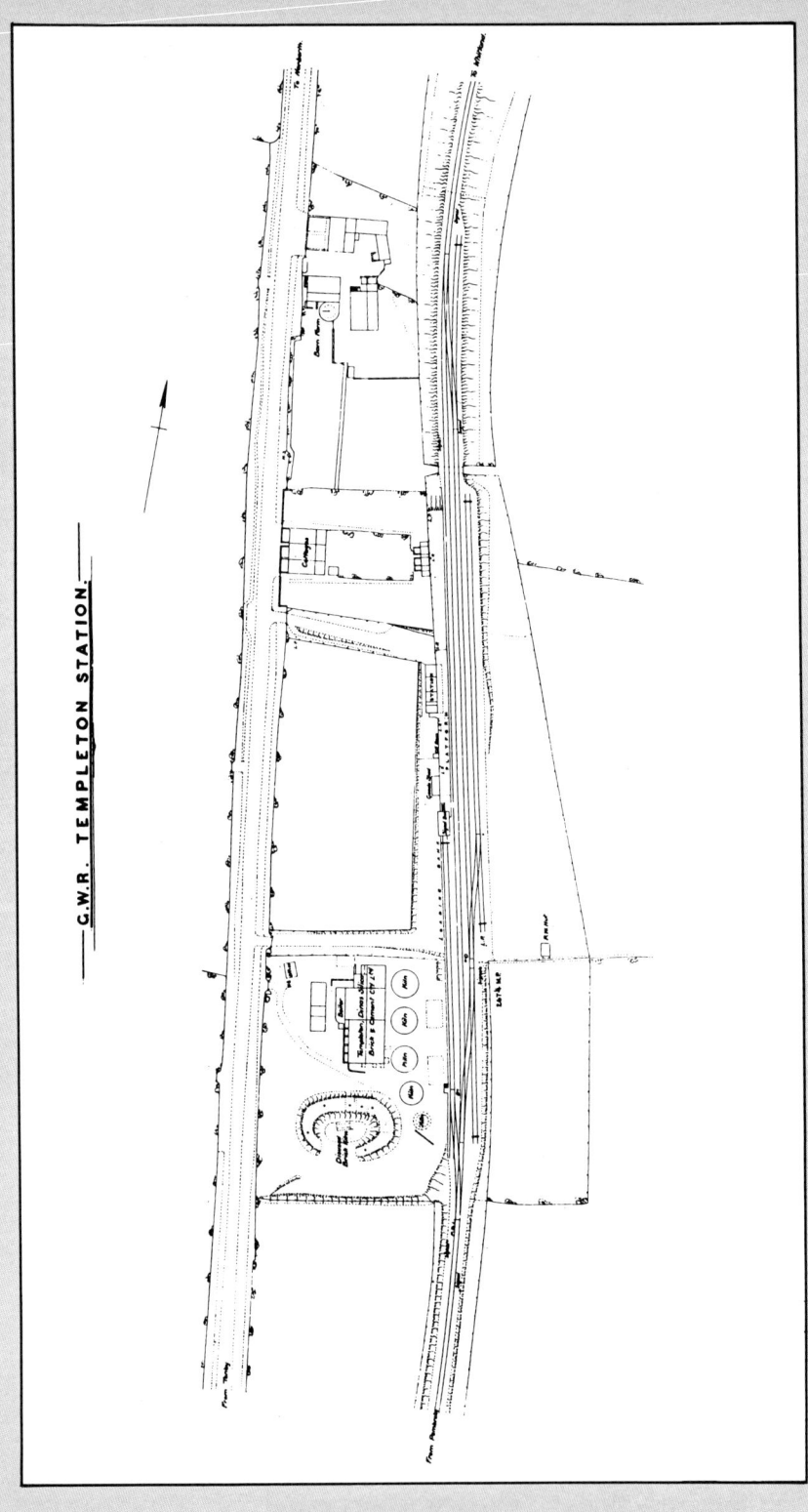

G.W.R. TEMPLETON STATION.

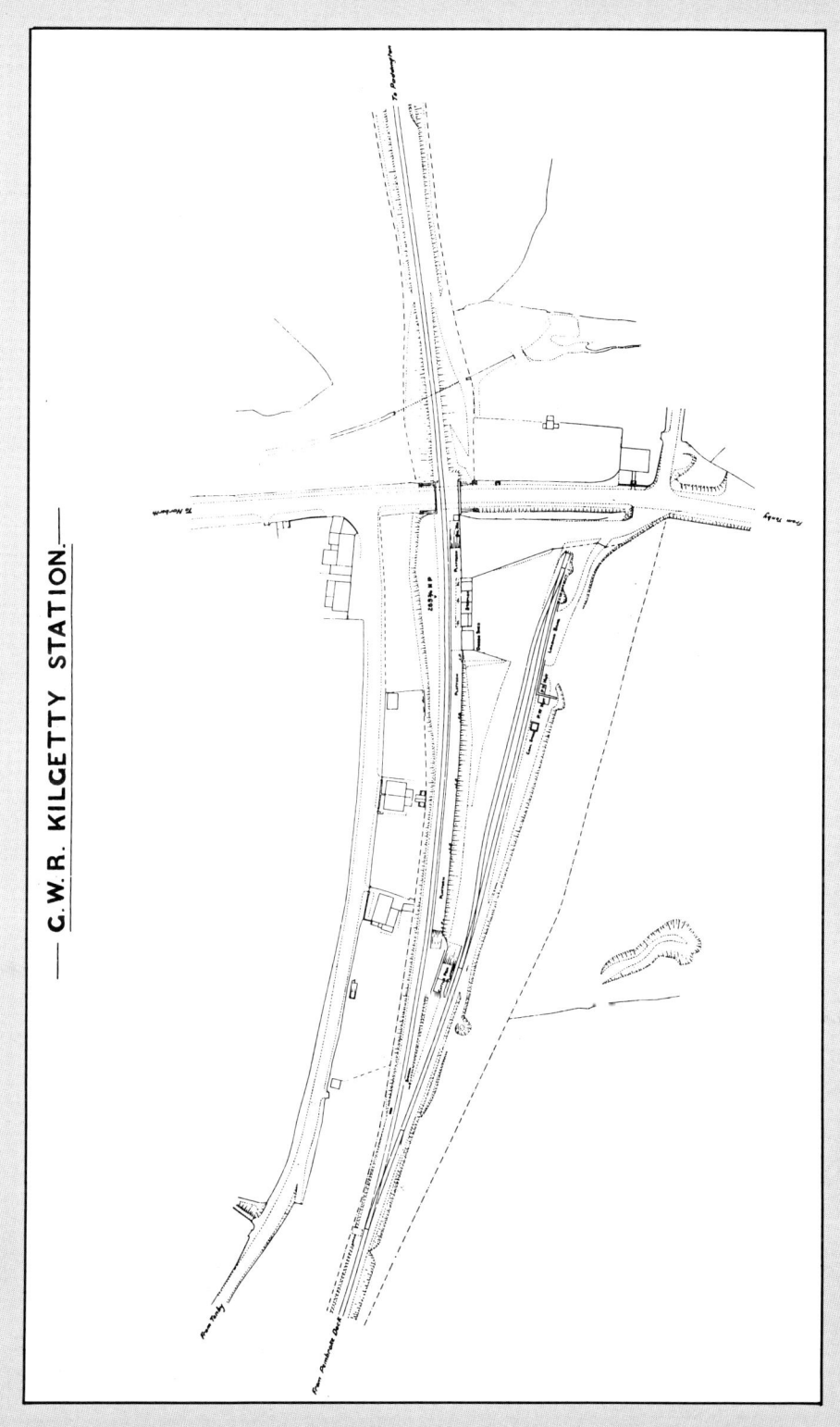

— G.W.R. KILGETTY STATION. —

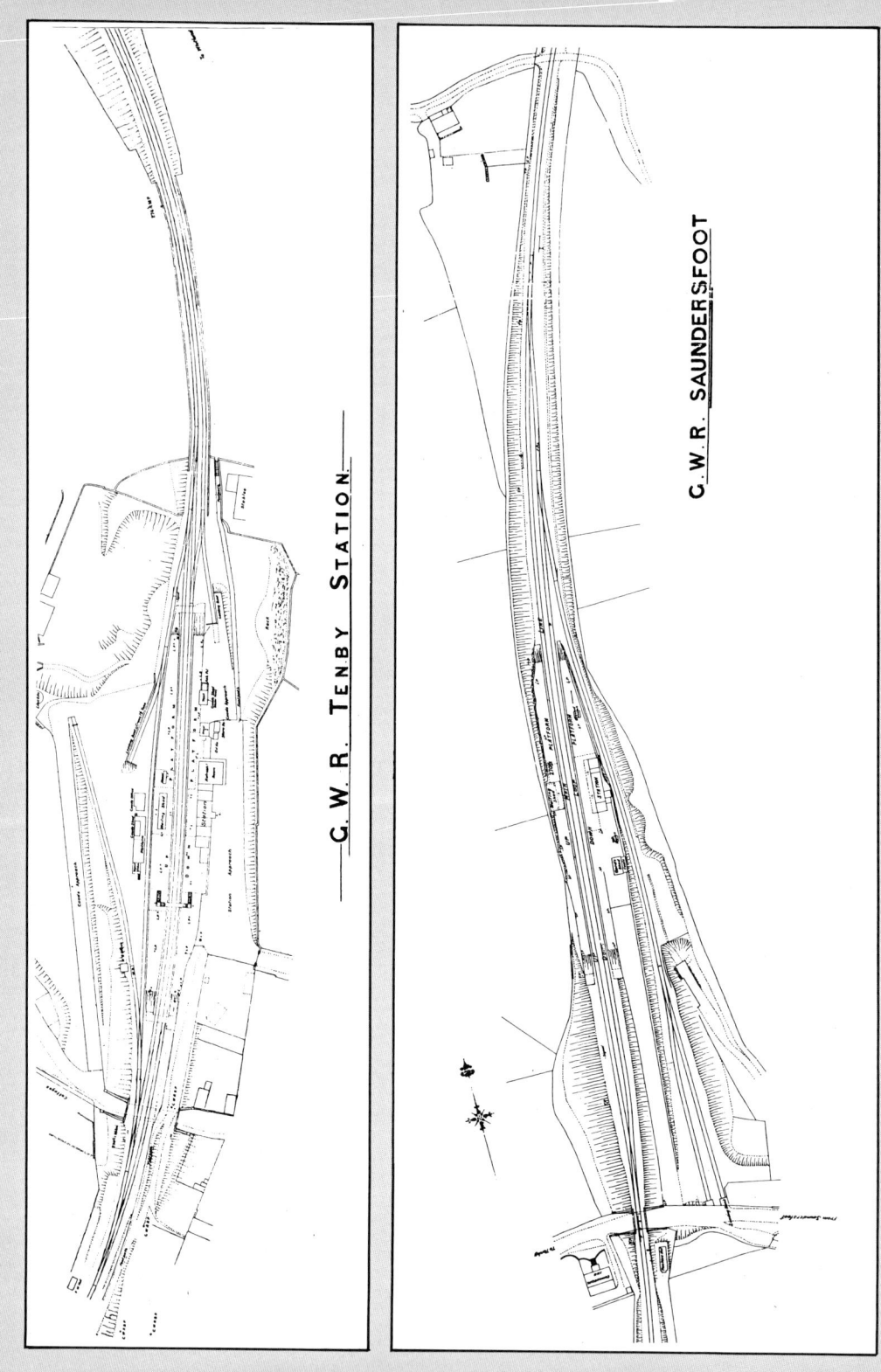

G.W.R. TENBY STATION.

G.W.R. SAUNDERSFOOT

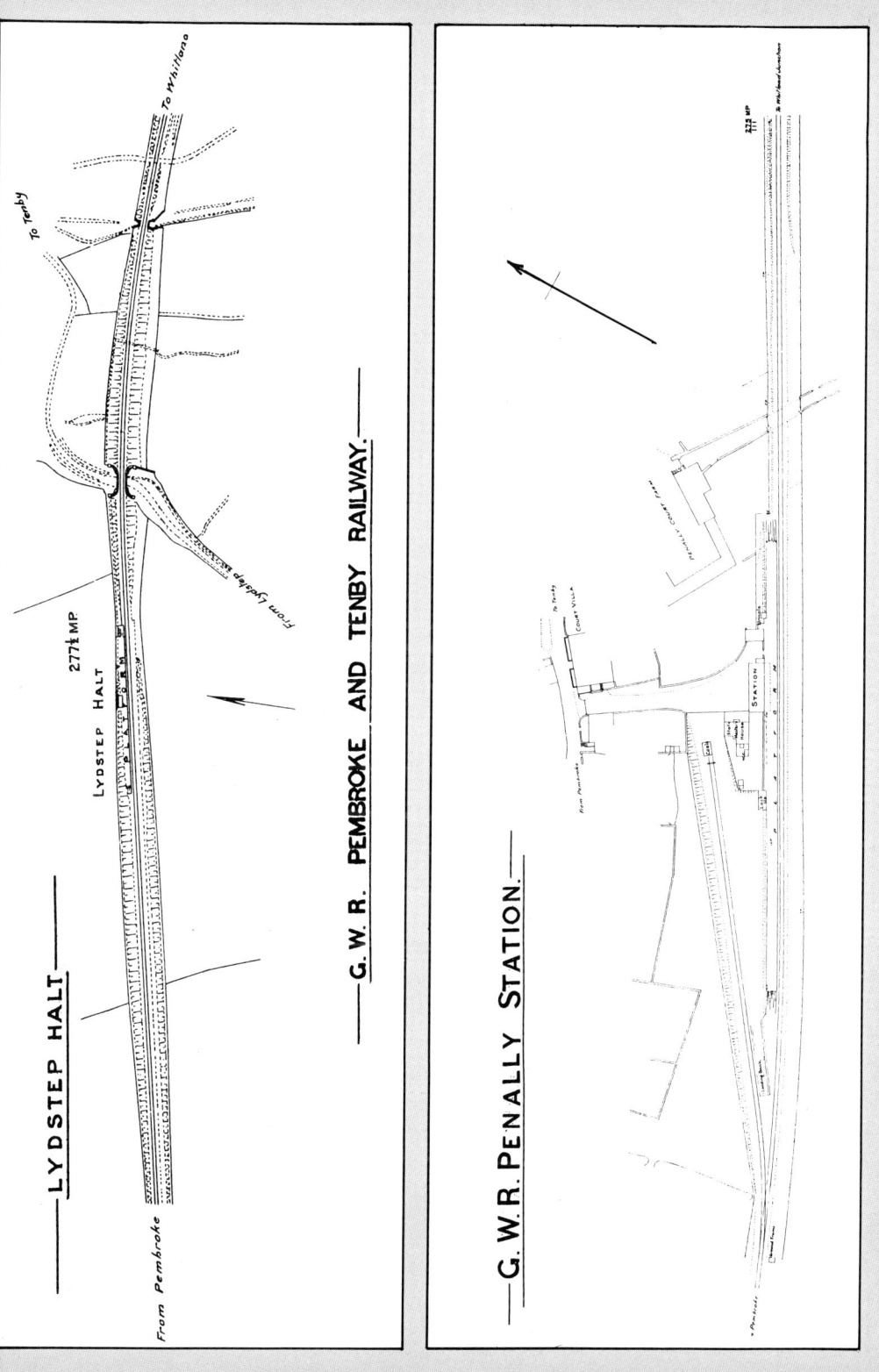

LYDSTEP HALT

To Whitland

To Tenby

277¼ MP.

LYDSTEP HALT

Lydstep Halt

From Lydstep

From Pembroke

—— G.W.R. PEMBROKE AND TENBY RAILWAY. ——

—— G.W.R. PENALLY STATION. ——

To Tenby

Court Villa

Penally Court Farm

STATION

From Pembroke

272 MP.

To Whitland Junction

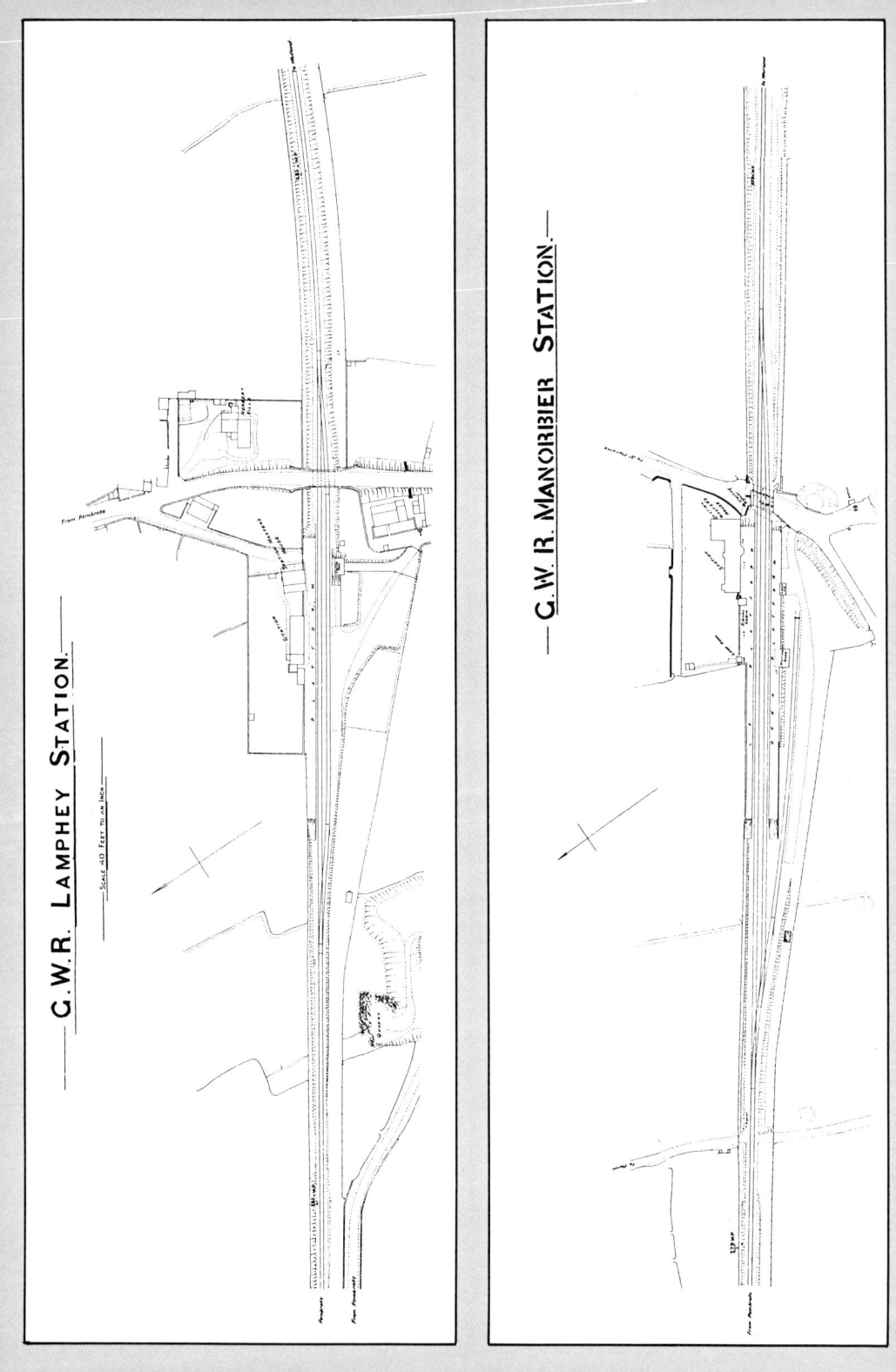

— G.W.R. LAMPHEY STATION. —

Scale 40 Feet to an Inch

— G.W.R. MANORBIER STATION. —

— G.W.R. PEMBROKE STATION. —

Scale 40 Feet to an Inch

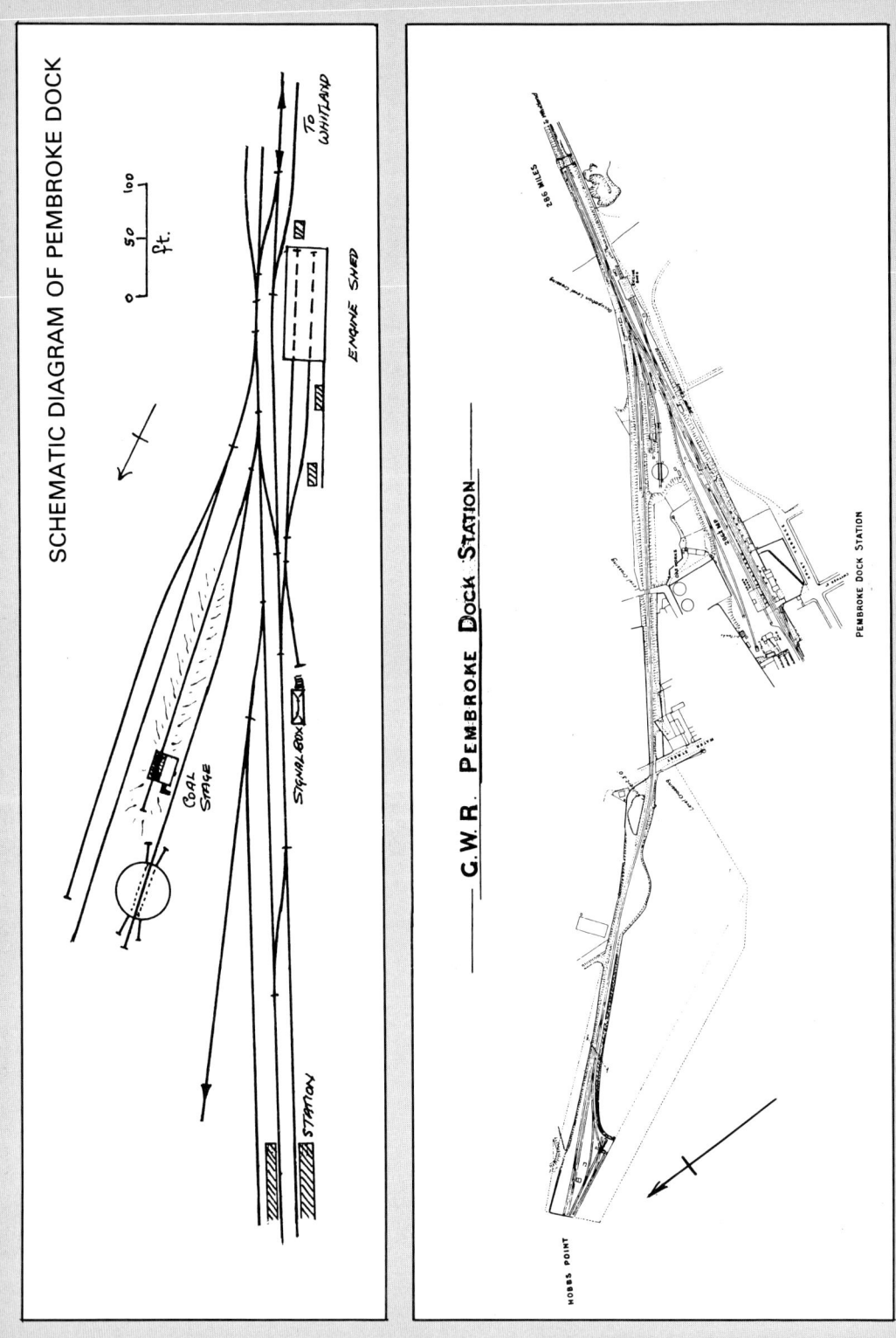

SCHEMATIC DIAGRAM OF PEMBROKE DOCK

TO WHITLAND

ENGINE SHED

COAL STAGE

SIGNAL BOX

STATION

0   50   100
ft.

G.W.R. PEMBROKE DOCK STATION

286 MILES

PEMBROKE DOCK STATION

HOBBS POINT

Carmarthen station, 14th August, 1964. 10.00 am DMU to Pembroke Dock pulls out. *M.R.C. Price*

DMU from Carmarthen enters Whitland. *M.R.C. Price*

Whitland station, looking west *c*.1935.   *R.E. Bowen Collection*

Whitland station from the footbridge, *c*.1914.   *W. Griffiths Collection*

No. 7804 *Baydon Manor* at Whitland with the down Pembroke Coast Express, 9th August, 1963.   *M.R.C. Price*

Whitland locomotive shed, with Mogul No. 7318 in the foreground on 22nd November, 1938.   *British Rail*

English Electric Type 3 D6931 pauses at Narberth station with an up freight on 13th August, 1965.   *M.R.C. Price*

Narberth station, looking north, *c.*1906.   *R.E. Bowen Collection*

Station, Narberth

Templeton station, *c*.1910.

R.E. Bowen Collection

Tablet exchange at Templeton, as No. D6931 heads north on freight, 13th August, 1965.

M.R.C. Price

Kilgetty station, looking south.   *O.P.C. Collection*

DMU train for Pembroke Dock enters Kilgetty station on the 25th August, 1966.   *M.R.C. Price*

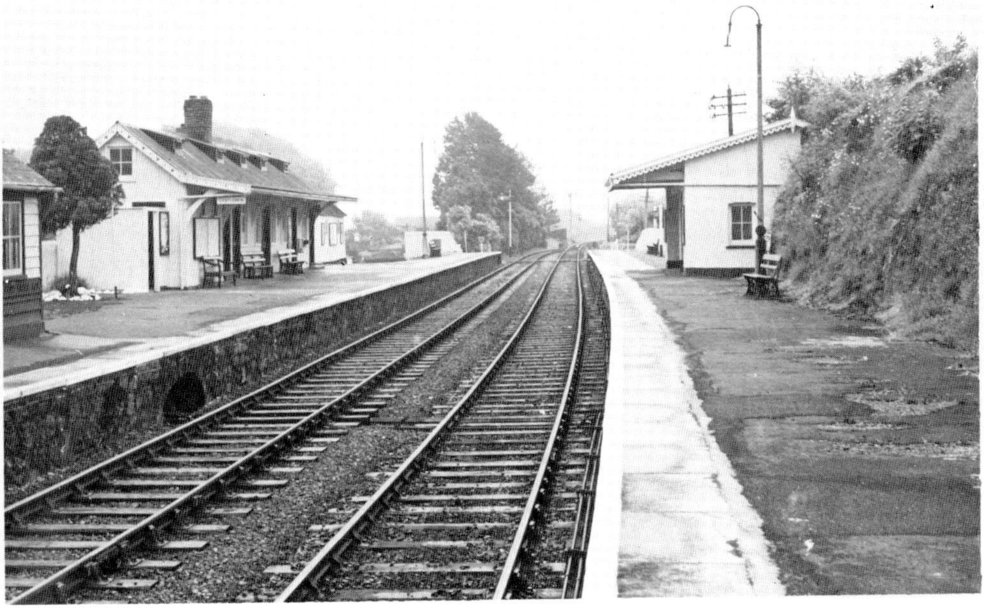

Saundersfoot station, looking south. *O.P.C. Collection*

Saundersfoot station, *c.*1914. *R. Howells Collection*

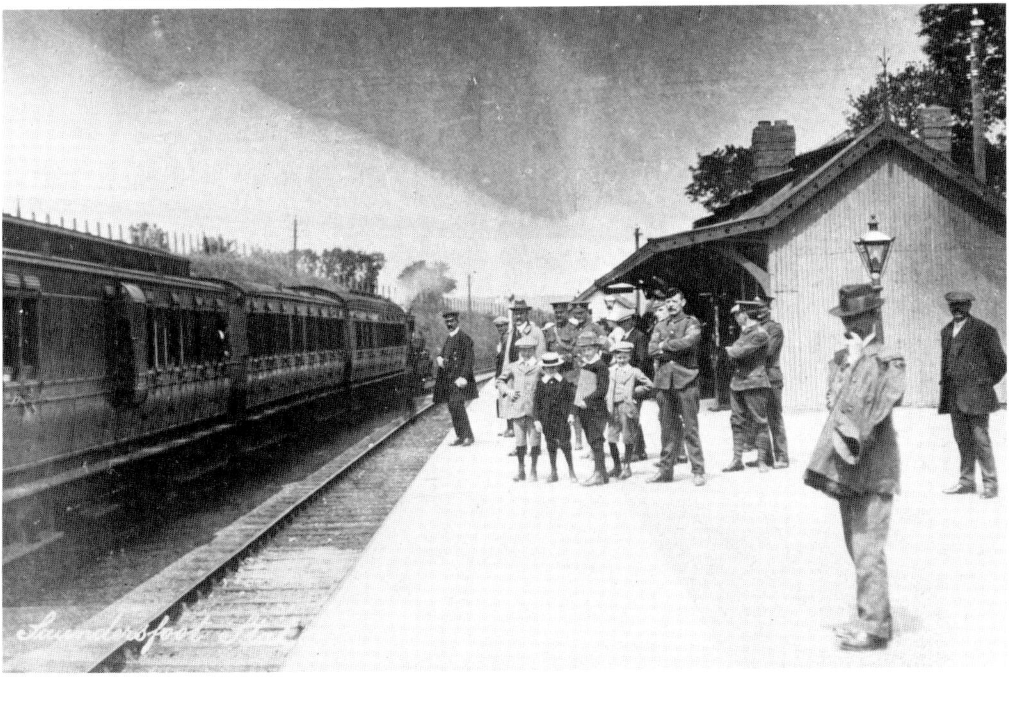

The ornate P & TR building on the down platform, Tenby. *S.C. Jenkins*

An Edwardian scene at Tenby station. *L.G.R.P., Courtesy David & Charles*

Prairie tanks at Tenby: 61xx 2–6–2T No. 6118 enters the station with a train from Pembroke Dock, and 41xx 2–6–2T No. 4132 waits in the loop with a parcels train on the 6th August, 1963.   *M.R.C. Price*

English Electric Type 3 No. D6921 shunts at Tenby, 12th August, 1964.
                                                           M.R.C. Price

Penally station, looking south.   *Lens of Sutton*

No. 7804 *Baydon Manor* pulls away from Penally with a Pembroke Dock train
on 14th August, 1963.   *M.R.C. Price*

Lydstep halt, (*left*) looking west, 13th August, 1964.　*M.R.C. Price*

Trains crossing at Manorbier: 73xx 2–6–0 No. 7332 arrives on a passenger train from Pembroke Dock.　*M.R.C. Price*

Manorbier station, looking east.　　　　　　*Lens of Sutton*

Beavers Hill halt, looking west.   *Lens of Sutton*

Lamphey station   *Lens of Sutton*

Lamphey station, looking east, 11th August, 1964. *M.R.C. Price*

Lamphey station, looking west. *O.P.C. Collection*

Pembroke, view east towards goods yard. *O.P.C. Collection*

Pembroke station, looking west. *Lens of Sutton*

Pembroke station, looking east.   *Lens of Sutton*

Pembroke Dock, looking east towards signalbox.   *Lens of Sutton*

Class 41xx 2–6–2T No. 4132 receives attention on arrival at Pembroke Dock on 9th August, 1963. *M.R.C. Price*

A DMU train awaits departure for Whitland from Pembroke Dock on 7th August, 1975. *M.R.C. Price*

Chapter Two
Origins

In the first half of the nineteenth century the town of Tenby, in the south east corner of Pembrokeshire, was not an especially easy place to visit. For generations the sea provided the most natural means of communication to and from the town, as for many other places in the county. Small vessels sailed from Bristol to Tenby twice a month, but in bad weather the wretched travellers might spend days tossing about in the Bristol Channel. The local roads were appalling, but gradual improvements eventually enabled a coach to operate, supposedly daily, bringing London within an uncomfortable thirty hours journey. At the same time, in the 1830s, significant road improvements were carried out between Carmarthen and Pater, or Pembroke Dock, after surveys directed by Thomas Telford. In 1814 Pembroke Dock had become the site for a Royal Naval dockyard, and in 1830–1832 a pier was constructed nearby at West Llanion, or Hobbs Point, to provide for a packetboat service to Ireland. It was not until the construction of the South Wales Railway that further improvements in communications became possible.

The South Wales Railway was incorporated in 1845 to build a railway from Gloucester via Cardiff, Swansea and Carmarthen to an entirely new Irish packet port to be built near Fishguard. A branch line was to run from the vicinity of Whitland direct to Pembroke Dock, by-passing Tenby. The SWR's authorised capital was initially £2,800,000 of which the Great Western Railway was intended to subscribe £600,000. The Act included powers to sell or lease the concern to the GWR which was also empowered to appoint six of the eighteen Directors. The influence of the Great Western, and the appointment of Isambard Kingdom Brunel as the SWR's Engineer, ensured that the railway would be built to his broad gauge of 7′ 0¼″. Construction began, and soon after, in December 1846, an agreement was reached whereby the GWR would lease the SWR on the completion of its entire line, any portion opening sooner being worked by the GWR on behalf of the South Wales company.

This agreement became a source of bitter controversy. Building took time, money was short, and partly as a result of the Irish famine of 1846 it became clear that the railway to Fishguard could not pay. In 1847 work on the SWR in west Wales was halted, but the Great Western would not compromise on the terms of the lease. The ensuing argument rumbled on until March 1851, nine months after the Chepstow–Swansea section of the line opened for traffic. The parties then agreed that the SWR should be completed to Milford Haven rather than Fishguard, and that the line should be managed by a joint committee of ten Directors, five from each company. In addition the South Wales was to provide accommodation for traffic, and the Great Western the locomotives and rolling stock to work it. A 999 year lease of the line by the GWR came into effect on 19th July, 1852, on the completion of the Wye bridge at Chepstow, the last link in the SWR between Gloucester and Swansea.

From the outset the South Wales Railway never regarded the Pembroke Dock branch as a top priority, and its attitude did not change. The company now decided to approach Milford Haven from the north, and forsaking the uncompleted earthworks of the Fishguard line at Clarbeston Road (then known as Cross Inn) it built a short line to Haverfordwest under powers obtained in an Act of 1846. The railway to Haverfordwest was opened on 2nd January, 1854, the route having been extended from Swansea to Carmarthen on 11th October, 1852. On Brunel's recommendation the SWR decided to make its terminus at the tiny fishing village of Neyland, just across the Haven from Pembroke Dock. This spot offered good shelter and deep water close to shore at all states of the tide. Accordingly in 1852 the South Wales company obtained Parliamentary approval for an extension from Haverfordwest to Neyland, and the line was opened on 15th April, 1856. The large South Wales Hotel was built near the terminus, and almost immediately a twice-weekly steamer service was started between Neyland and Waterford. It was operated for some years by Messrs Ford & Jackson.

The citizens of the small town of Milford, three miles further west, were annoyed to discover that the new terminus had claimed the name "Milford Haven". However, in 1859, when plans were afoot for Milford to have its own branch railway, the station was renamed "Neyland". Very soon after this was changed to "New Milford", and it was with this title that the place became famous as the packet port for Ireland.

In the meantime inhabitants of the southern parts of Pembrokeshire were becoming restless at the postponement of plans to build a branch to Pembroke Dock. The delay was particularly aggravating for the owners of land and minerals in the neighbourhood of Saundersfoot who were energetically exploiting the local coal measures and ironstone. As early as 1829 Parliament had authorised the Saundersfoot Railway, a 4ft gauge tramroad worked by horses connecting some of the collieries with a new harbour at Saundersfoot. This concern began trading officially on 1st March, 1834, and within a few years it comprised a 4½ mile line from Saundersfoot inland to Thomas Chapel, and a branch running north along the coast to Wiseman's Bridge, and then on to collieries at Stepaside and Kilgetty.

The Chairman of the Saundersfoot Railway & Harbour Co, and the principal shareholder, was Sir Richard Bulkeley Philipps. In 1845,

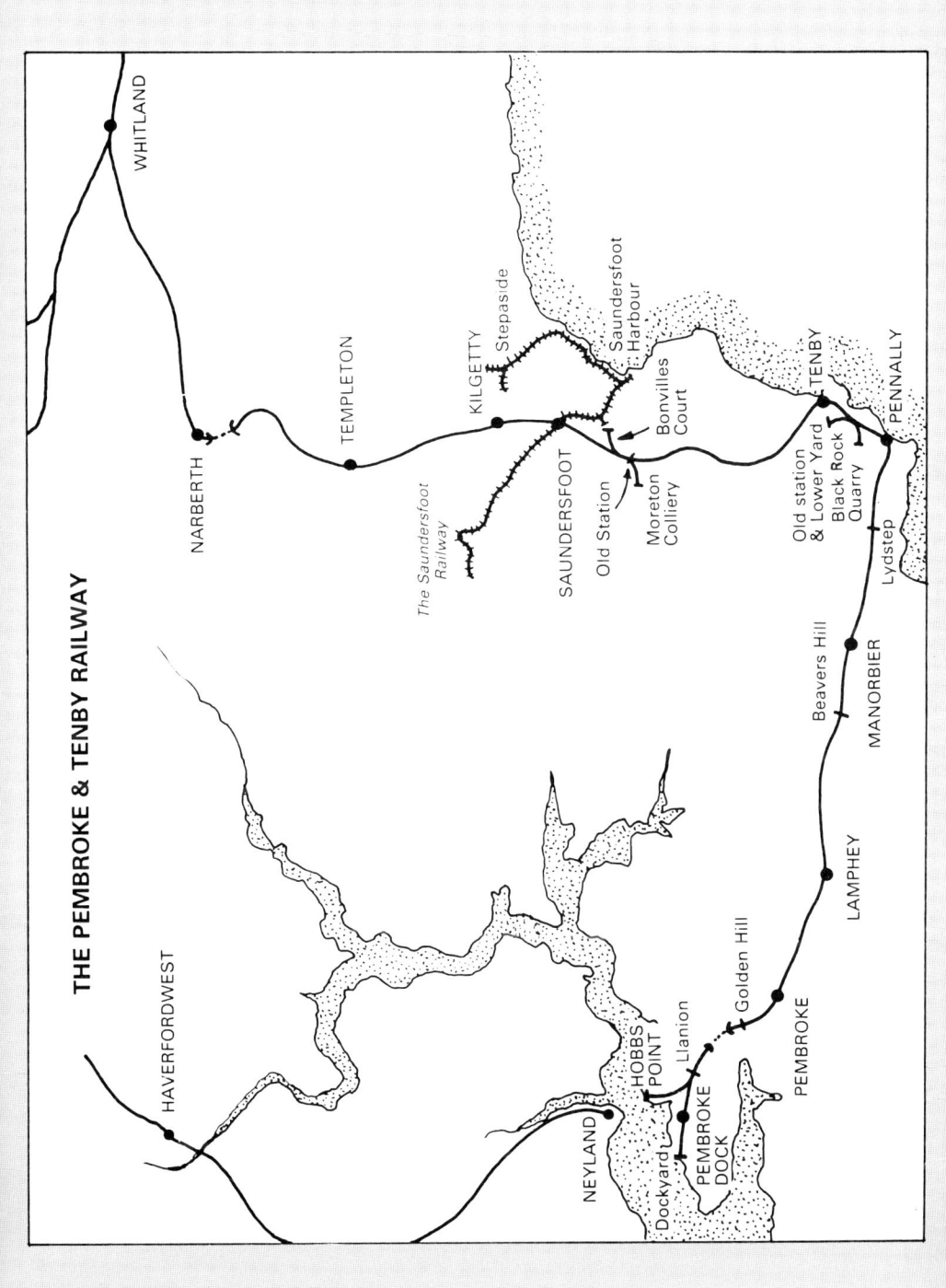

THE PEMBROKE & TENBY RAILWAY

WHITLAND

TEMPLETON

NARBERTH

KILGETTY

Stepaside

Saundersfoot
Harbour

Bonvilles
Court

SAUNDERSFOOT

Old Station

*The Saundersfoot
Railway*

Moreton
Colliery

TENBY

PENNALLY

Old station
& Lower Yard
Black Rock
Quarry

Lydstep

Beavers Hill

MANORBIER

LAMPHEY

HAVERFORDWEST

Golden Hill

Llanion

HOBBS
POINT

PEMBROKE

NEYLAND

Dockyard

PEMBROKE
DOCK

when the SWR was authorised, he and his colleagues decided to seek powers to build a railway linking both Tenby and Saundersfoot to the line of the proposed Pembroke Dock branch at the village of Reynalton. The project was plainly intended to improve facilities for moving local anthracite coal, and indeed part of the route followed the alignment of a section of the Saundersfoot Railway's Thomas Chapel line. The Engineer of this scheme, Francis Giles, estimated the costs at £140,000. Although the project was authorised in 1846 as the Tenby, Saundersfoot and South Wales Railway and Pier Co, with Sir R.B. Philipps as the largest individual shareholder, its progress was quickly checked in 1847 when work stopped on the SWR in West Wales. In the event, as the Pembroke Dock branch was not started, the TS&SWR&P was not started either, and the development of railways in the area eventually took quite a different course to that contemplated in 1846.

When the South Wales Railway was opened to Haverfordwest on 2nd January, 1854, a station was established at Narberth Road, about three miles north of the small town of Narberth. Very soon a coach service was provided between this station and Tenby over fourteen miles of rough and hilly roads. The naturalist Phillip Gosse travelled to Tenby by this route, and in 1856 he published a colourful account of the journey.

> "Narbeth Road and Tenby!" shouts the guard as he runs along the train; and up we jump, snatch up umbrellas, cloaks and carpet bags, and hastily get out, glad to escape from our imprisonment, a seven hours endurance of that renowned prescription "when taken to be well shaken".

The next difficulty for Gosse "was how to choose between the pretensions of the eager coachmen . . . their intense earnestness and rivalry were most laughable". Having decided to take the coach destined for the Cobourg Hotel rather than that for the White Lion, Gosse observed that both were so well loaded that "the coachies might have spared their greed". However, the four-in-hand vehicle was now away, and "it was a pleasant change from the railway carriage to the outside of a coach, on a brilliant summer evening, driving up hill and down dell between hedges green with foliage and with flowers". Passing through the villages it seemed that the whole population turned out to line the street — "for the transit of the Tenby coaches was evidently the Great Exhibition of the day".

One of the coaches on the Narberth Road–Tenby run at this period was the North Mail coach, administered by the Post Office authorities. In 1854 it ran on weekdays only (including Saturdays) leaving Tenby at 7.30 am and arriving at Narberth Road at 9.25 am after stops at Begelly (8.10 am) and Narberth (8.55 am). The train to Carmarthen departed at 9.45 am. In the opposite direction the train from Carmarthen reached Narberth Road at 1.38 pm. The coach departed at 2.00 pm and reached Narberth at 2.30 pm, Begelly at 3.25 pm and Tenby at 4.05 pm.

Whilst the South Wales Railway was losing interest in the Pembroke Dock branch, others were not. In 1852 a local landowner, Baron de Rutzen, went to court for a writ of mandamus to compel the company to complete the line. He was pacified by the SWR's promise to introduce a new Bill for the branch. Meanwhile another landowner, Mr Kinderly, joined the South Wales Board and urged the company to go ahead. He did so with good reason. In the autumn of 1852 he and Mr Wythes, part owner of an estate in Pembroke, helped to promote a scheme for the building of docks at Pennar Gut, to the west of Pembroke, envisaging also a rail link to the Pembroke Dock branch. Under pressure the SWR in 1853 sought a time extension for the branch, with powers to build it by a shorter route running closer to Tenby, and adding an extension from Pembroke to Pennar Gut.

This Bill duly went before Parliament, and as it did so the Cardwell clause was introduced into railway Bills, making it possible to penalise companies failing to complete their lines by the suspension of dividend payments. Not unnaturally the SWR had second thoughts but Wythes, Kinderly and others again pressed the company to continue. Mr Wythes, in partnership with Mr Treadwell, a prominent contractor, actually offered to build the railway, taking shares in payment, the interest on which was to be guaranteed out of profits on the new branch and not on the company's other funds. This allayed the SWR's anxieties, and the 1853 Bill was steered through Parliament. Hardly had this been achieved before problems arose. Although the docks were a vital part of the scheme, little or nothing was done about building them. Accordingly nothing was done about building the branch either. Wythes and Treadwell's part in this delay is far from clear, but in 1854, when the SWR attempted to enforce their agreement in the Court of Chancery, the contractors showed skill in the art of commercial escapology, and wriggled free. Not only was the company unsuccessful, but it was now ensnared in the trap of the Cardwell clause. Well aware of its difficult position the South Wales company went to Parliament for power to abandon the Pembroke Dock branch and the Pennar extension. The company claimed it had made a bona fide attempt to enforce the contract against Wythes & Treadwell, and stated that it had no funds with which to make the line. This argument impressed neither the Pembrokeshire landowners nor the Admiralty, both of which stood to benefit by the railway. They opposed the Bill and in 1855 it was thrown out.

After this setback powers to construct a large portion of the

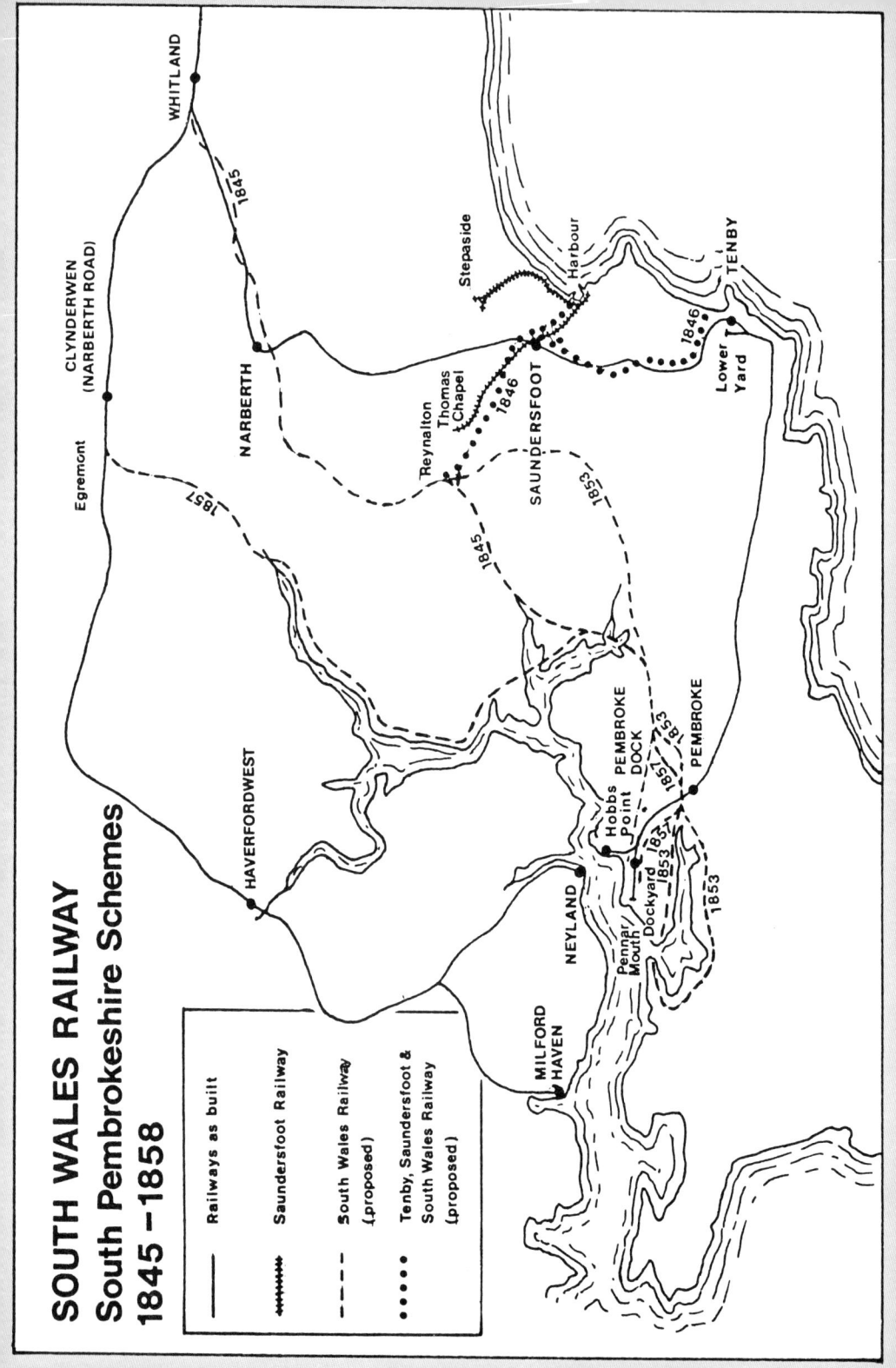

SOUTH WALES RAILWAY
South Pembrokeshire Schemes
1845–1858

Railways as built

Saundersfoot Railway

South Wales Railway
(proposed)

Tenby, Saundersfoot &
South Wales Railway
(proposed)

WHITLAND

CLYNDERWEN
(NARBERTH ROAD)

Egremont

NARBERTH

Stepaside

Harbour

TENBY

1845

1846

Reynalton

Thomas
Chapel

SAUNDERSFOOT

1846

Lower
Yard

1857

1845

1853

HAVERFORDWEST

PEMBROKE
DOCK

1853

PEMBROKE

Hobbs
Point

NEYLAND

Pennar
Mouth

Dockyard

1853

1853

1853

MILFORD
HAVEN

Pembroke line expired in 1856, and the rest in 1858, whilst the company continued to say that it had no means to complete the works. The local landowners felt frustrated and angry. In 1857, one of them, Nicholas Adamson Roch, involved the company in litigation and so persuaded the SWR to apply to Parliament for new powers to build the Pembroke Dock branch. Put on the spot in this way, the company responded with deceptive cunning. In the next session it went to Parliament with two Bills, not one. The first was to renew powers for the branch from Whitland, and the other was for an alternative and shorter branch to Pembroke Dock following the east bank of the River Cleddau from Egremont, near Narberth Road, on the main line. These routes became known as the Whitland line and the Egremont line respectively. Although the company insisted that both Bills were prepared in good faith, to test which line would be suited to the needs of the district, Pembrokeshire people were suspicious. Such a concern for the neighbourhood had not been characteristic of the company, and even the SWR's claim that the Egremont line would save £60,000 did not convince popular opinion of the company's sincerity. Before long local fears were seen to be justified.

The Egremont line was surveyed in 1857 by John Fowler, acting in place of Brunel who had bigger tasks to tackle elsewhere. The route, 19 miles 5 chains long, was so sinuous it was not a lot shorter than the Whitland line, and it may be wondered if it was really much cheaper. The Egremont route crossed several creeks and pills of the Cleddau and at Landshipping, for example, it required some heavy engineering. Apart from Pembroke Dock itself it served no significant centres of population, passing some distance away from Narberth and Pembroke. It was also too far west to be of any help to the coal owners of the Saundersfoot area. In the circumstances complaints were hardly surprising. In February 1858 Mr Allen, described as "a shareholder with a £100 stack" obtained an injunction to suspend the SWR's dividends for the second half of 1857 because he thought it a breach of faith for the company to apply for both lines. This action may have relieved his temper, but it achieved no more. The House of Commons, with an eye on expense, rejected the Whitland line leaving the House of Lords free to consider the Egremont line only.

The Bill for the Egremont line came before the Select Committee of the House of Lords on 16th July, 1858. F.G. Saunders, Secretary of the SWR, recalled the history of the issue at some length, and under cross-examination admitted that "but for the compulsion under which they found themselves the Directors did not want to make either line to Pembroke, because for a number of years they did not think it would be remunerative". After repeating that the Directors were bona fide in their intention to build the branch if sanctioned,

Saunders confirmed that cost was the main pressure. Mentioning that the SWR had powers to build the counsel cross-examining retorted "you state to their Lordships that you have power to raise the amount of £350,000 — you have never put a spade into the ground upon the Whitland Line". Saunders had to admit it, and this must have influenced the Committee. A number of other witnesses appeared, mostly to criticise the Bill, and in due course it was rejected. However, the Committee did not listen too closely to all the critics: in making its decision it declared that the Egremont line was the cheapest and best which the country allowed, but the population was insufficient to justify the expense. Accordingly the SWR was spared responsibility for building the branch, and there can be little doubt that it was greatly relieved.

304.—PEMBROKE AND TENBY.

Incorporated by 22 and 23 Vic., cap. 6 (21st July, 1859), to make railways from Pembroke Dock to Tenby, and from the former place to Hobb's Point. Capital, 80,000l. in 10l. shares; loans, 26, 600l. Length of first line, to commence at or near Pembroke Docks and to terminate at Tenby, 11¾ miles ; and length of second, to commence at or near Pembroke Docks and to terminate at Hobb's Point, two furlongs and 7½ chains. Estimate, 80,000l. Opened, 27½ miles.

By 27 and 28 Vic., cap. 183 (14th July, 1864), the company was authorised to construct several short lines, including an extension to Whitland. Length, 18 miles. Capital, 200,000l. in shares, and 66,000l. on loan.

By 29 and 30 Vic., cap. 330 (6th August, 1866), the company was authorised to extend the line to Carmarthen and to Milford Haven. Length, 15¾ miles. Capital, 200 000l. in shares, and 65,600l. on loan. Arrangements with Great Western, Cambrian, Central Wales, Llanelly, and Manchester and Milford. By arrangements with the lessees, the dividends are at the rate of 5 per cent. per annum.

It was reported in August that the traffic continued to increase, the half-year's earnings being 2,375l. in excess of the corresponding period, while the working expenses had only increased 499l. The narrow gauge line between Whitland and Carmarthen had been opened, from which a considerable addition to revenue was anticipated.

CAPITAL.—The receipts and expenditure on this account to 30th June, 1869, have been as follow :—

Received.		*Expended.*	
Shares and stock	£237,066	On lines opened for traffic, including 20,000l. paid to Great Western, for converting 14 miles of their broad gauge line between Whitland and Carmarthen into narrow gauge	£323,209
Loans	107,785		
Debenture stock	2,000		
Receipts on forfeited shares	28		
Rent-charges capitalised at 20 year's purchase	3,160	Working stock	26,829
	£350,039		£350,039

Meetings in February and August.

No. of Directors—7 ; minimum, 5; quorum, 3. *Qualification*, 300l.

DIRECTORS :

Chairman—WILLIAM OWEN, Esq., Whitby Bush, Haverfordwest,
Deputy-Chairman—JOHN JAMES BARROW, Esq., Normanton Hall, Southwell, Notts.

G. E. Forster, Esq., Uppingham, Rutland. | F. L. Clark, Esq., Pembroke.
Stephen Robinson, Esq., The Moor, Kington, Herefordshire. | John Barrow, Esq., Ringwood, Chesterfield.

OFFICERS.—Sec., Thomas Stokes, Pembroke Dock ; Traffic Man., Isaac Smedley, Pembroke Dock ; Eng., J. W. Szlumper; Auditors, R. Greenish, Haverfordwest, and J. Phelps, Tenby ; Solicitor, Wm. Davies, Haverfordwest.
Offices—Pembroke Dock.

Extract from Bradshaw Railway Manual of 1870.

Chapter Three

Building the Pembroke & Tenby

The failure of the SWR's 1858 Bills came as a considerable disappointment to many south Pembrokeshire people. Disillusioned with the SWR some of them decided to promote their own line on the south side of the Milford Haven. They wasted little time, and on 21st July, 1859, the South Wales, Pembroke and Tenby Junction railway was incorporated by Act of Parliament. This line was 11½ miles long, with a route elaborately described as ". . . commencing not less than one furlong eastward of the western most fence of the garden near the town of Pembroke Dock, abutting on the public road leading from Pembroke to Hobbs Point, which garden is the property of Thomas Meyrick Esq . . . and terminating at the Town Quarry, near the town of Tenby". Provision was also made for a short line from the garden so mentioned to the pier at Hobbs Point, and to judge from the plans this line was to be an extension of the main railway, rather than a branch from it.

The Chairman of the railway company was William Owen of Haverfordwest, and the first Directors were Stephen Lewis, Edward Septimus Codd, George Beauchamp Cole, Thomas Jackson, James Baird Burke and George Edward Adams. At the time of the Act the railway's Engineer was J.S. Burke, but in February 1860, he was replaced by James Mathias. The company had an authorised capital of £80,000 with borrowing powers for a further £26,000. In both title and drafting the Act suggests that initially the railway was regarded more as an extension from the SWR at Neyland than as a potential new link with the South Wales main line. This impression is increased by the fact that the SWP&TJR was authorised as a 4' 8½" gauge railway and not as a broad gauge route. Even so, there was very soon talk of extending the line from Tenby to the SWR at Whitland.

Such talk remained talk for several years. By October, 1859, subscriptions amounted to less than £7000, and in the following months more than one shareholders' meeting was cancelled for want of a quorum. Even though the inspiration for the project was now local, some landowners persisted in their hostility, preferring either some scheme of their own, or no railway at all. For a couple of years it looked doubtful if construction would ever start. The first available minute of Board meetings, dated 3rd July, 1861, indicates that by then little had been accomplished beyond a change of company name to the simpler title "Pembroke and Tenby Railway". On this occasion the meeting was held at the Castle Hotel, Pembroke, under the chairmanship of William Owen. It dealt with a few minor matters. A week later, however, the Chairman and two other Directors, Lewis Mathias and Thomas Jackson, met at the South Wales Hotel, Neyland, and decided to seek possession of land at their own expense. The company was stirring at last, although subscriptions were coming in slowly.

By August, 1861, James Mathias was revising working plans for use by a contractor, tenders having been received from "respectable and responsible contractors". One of these was Richard Hattersley who was contractor to the Central Wales Railway. Another was David Davies of Llandinam, already notable as contractor to several railway companies in North and Mid Wales. On his first visit to Tenby he decided that the district could support a railway. Accordingly, in partnership with his friend Ezra Roberts of St. Asaph, Denbighshire, he made a bid to become contractor to the P&TR. Whereas Hattersley insisted that a proportion of the capital be raised by independent subscription before any work began, Davies and Roberts made no such stipulation. They indicated that they were ready to put up a very large part of the capital themselves. In the circumstances it was almost inevitable that they would get the job, but misunderstandings arose, and for several months in 1862 Hattersley maintained he had a contract. The P&T consistently resisted his claims, and the row died down when turned over to the lawyers to settle.

On 4th July, 1862, the P&T Board sealed an agreement giving Davies & Roberts complete responsibility for making the line. For the sum of £106,600 the contractors agreed to complete the railway, including stations and accommodation works, to the specification of the company's Engineer and to the satisfaction of the Board of Trade. They also agreed to provide all the necessary rolling stock. In payment they were to receive the entire authorised capital of the company, comprising cash genuinely subscribed, and the balance in shares and debentures. Davies & Roberts undertook to complete the work by 21st July, 1864, and in the meantime agreed to advance money when required to complete the purchase of the necessary land.

By any reckoning this was a remarkable deal, but it has to be seen in the light of contemporary practice. In the 1850s and 1860s contractors frequently involved themselves in far more than construction work, sometimes playing a part in railway promotion, land purchase and the remuneration of solicitors and engineers. Payment in the company's shares and debentures was typical of the great era of contractors' lines. If a contractor assumed responsibility for finding the entire share capital he was usually enabled to put friends on to the Board in order to protect his interests. Thus the Pembroke & Tenby Railway became a fine example of a contractor's line: Davies & Roberts not only provided virtually all the capital but for seven years they actually operated the railway. One or two of the Directors —

Martin Smith of Denbigh, for example — were certainly contractor's friends. In the circumstances it is not surprising that throughout this period the company's own records are not very informative. The reason is simple. Davies & Roberts took most of the decisions!

On 16th July, 1862, the *Haverfordwest & Milford Haven Telegraph* reported that the contract had been let "to Messrs Davies & Roberts of Denbigh on favourable terms, the work to be commenced immediately". On 6th August the paper referred to the P&T getting over the "much and vexatious delay chiefly if not entirely caused by the unwise policy of certain landowners". By now the contractors were in the district, accompanied by workmen and the first instalment of their plant. They promptly took the hitherto limp and listless venture by the scruff of the neck, and stood it on its feet. On 5th September, 1862 the Engineer of the P&T "together with the Mayor and Town Council of Tenby" inspected the land required for Tenby station in anticipation of its development. On 22nd September the schooner *Pembroke* arrived at Tenby with contractors' plant, and two days later the *Telegraph* reported that a gang of navvies had been preparing a road to move the plant from Tenby's south beach to the line of the railway. Although most of the equipment and materials were delivered in this way, it is thought that some plant was provided in the Pembroke area as soon as work started there. Even so, owing to the heavy engineering required on the railway west of Pembroke, and problems in negotiations for government land at Hobbs Point, construction west of Pembroke was initially deferred.

Ironically, after the years of delay, at the very moment Davies & Roberts were getting a grip on the P&T scheme, they were confronted with rival railway projects. One or two appear to have been so much hot air — like the proposal of the impecunious Carmarthen & Cardigan Railway to link Milford Haven with Pencader, forty miles away across the Prescelly hills. More significant was a new and locally inspired plan to build a line direct from Whitland to Narberth, Begelly and Pembroke Dock. This echo of the abortive South Wales branch was the brainchild of disgruntled owners of land and mineral rights in the coalfield around Saundersfoot: its supporters included J.M. Child of Begelly House, Harcourt Powell, another Begelly property owner, and C.R. Vickerman, by now the Chairman of the Saundersfoot Railway & Harbour Co. In November, 1862, the *Haverfordwest & Milford Haven Telegraph* reported that in the next session of Parliament the promoters would seek powers to build their line, the Whitland & Milford Haven Railway. "During the past weeks" said the *Telegraph* on 19th November, "Engineers and surveyors have been busily engaged in laying out the line, and other parties have been equally busy preparing the references". The Engineer of the Whitland & Milford Haven Railway was

James Shipway, and by the end of the year he had estimated the cost of the line to be £240,000. Unfortunately for him, the survey seems to have been carried out with more speed than accuracy because it was said later that the levels were at fault. At any rate both the Carmarthen & Cardigan Railway and P&TR objected to the Bill, and in February, 1863, it was rejected, having failed to comply with standing orders. The W&MH promoters regarded the defeat as temporary, but it gave Davies & Roberts valuable time to demonstrate their ability to make the P&T take shape on the ground.

Construction of the Pembroke & Tenby was already well under way. On 27th February, 1863 the Directors told a half yearly meeting of shareholders that the contractors were making steady progress with the works in spite of bad weather. They saw "every prospect of the line being opened for public traffic between the towns of Tenby and Pembroke early in the summer". Davies & Roberts' progress in five months was remarkable. Some work had now started on the section between Pembroke and Pater (Pembroke Dock) including the shafts at each end of the tunnel at Golden Hill. Between Pembroke and Lamphey permanent rails had been laid down at formation level, and ballasting was about to begin. The bridge over the railway at Lamphey had just been started, but the next bridge, known as Cleggars Bridge, had been finished, and the embankment was about to be closed up to it. Further east three bridges still had to be completed, and work was continuing on some embankments. From the Penally embankment to Tenby the permanent rails were laid at formation level, and awaited ballasting. The Engineer concluded that "the greatest drawback is the deficiency of ballast", adding that "your contractors have already provided themselves with a dozen permanent ballast wagons, and will have an engine here in about a month".

The day the locomotive arrived in Tenby seems to have been an occasion for general celebration. The engine is believed to have been hauled over the fourteen rough miles from Narberth Road by a team of 33 horses. As it approached the town it was apparently greeted by the Tenby Volunteer Brass Band, who then accompanied the procession to the railway terminus at the green, where a large crowd was gathered. The event is said to have occurred on 6th May, 1863, but it may well have been earlier. Unfortunately a search of contemporary local newspapers has not enabled either the date of the facts to be confirmed. However, newspapers do indicate that a locomotive was in use by the end of May, but mostly on the section between Pembroke and Norchard, near Manorbier. Norchard, incidentally, was the scene of the P&T's first recorded fatal accident, on 21st March, 1863. That day a 15 year old boy who was leading horses hitched to spoil wagons was killed when run over by a loaded wagon.

On 17th June, 1863, the *Haverfordwest & Milford Haven Telegraph* published a report so colourful it deserves to be noted:

> The 12th inst was a day memorable in the annals of Tenby. On that day the engine that had been for some time running between Pembroke and Norchard ran through the whole course of the line to Tenby, arriving there at 6 o'clock p.m. and taking after it several trucks filled with people. On arriving at the bridge which spans the lake that divides the parishes of Penally and Tenby it was loudly cheered. The cheers were taken up by those on the wagons, and continued for some time . . . The thoughts of the people of Tenby in their highest elevation, a few years ago never reached such a height as that of a steam engine arriving in their town within so short a period, followed by twelve trucks laden with over 600 people of all ages and both sexes among whom were the men to whose energy and skill all is due — the contractors Messrs Davies & Roberts whose bright countenances seemed to say that though Tenby had slept for many long years the hour for action had come and this would raise her up.

Although the locomotive was not described it was almost certainly David Davies' own engine *Llandinam*. It is believed to have been used again on another public excursion some days later, but that occasion was apparently marred when a wagon was derailed and its solitary occupant thrown into a ditch! By now the opening of the line was approaching, and the *Telegraph*'s reporter in Tenby was striving to maintain the excitement. On 8th July he reported that workmen had been busy at Tenby station "fixing the turning table and laying points so as to enable one of the new engines to get under steam . . . for the first time since its arrival on 4th inst." Two tank locomotives ordered by the contractors from Sharp, Stewart & Co, had evidently arrived, and final preparations were being made for the Board of Trade inspection. This took place on 24th July, 1863, and approval was given for the railway to open to public traffic on Thursday 30th July, 1863.

The opening day was a general holiday in both Pembroke and Tenby, and began with the ringing of bells and other joyful demonstrations. Public buildings were gaily decorated with flags and streamers, and principal streets were bridged at intervals with arches of evergreens. According to the Traffic Managers' publicity twelve trains ran each way, the first leaving Tenby at 7.30 am, the official opening train left Pembroke at noon carrying the Directors of the company, the Mayor, Town Clerk and corporation of Pembroke, the High Sheriff of Pembrokeshire and the Mayor of Haverfordwest and other gentlemen. Crowds greeted the train at different places along the line, and at Tenby the Directors were met by the Mayor and Corporation who congratulated them on the success of the undertaking. Amid more crowds the dignitaries then adjourned to the Market

House where a public breakfast was "served up in most excellent style, the building having been tastefully and elegantly decorated for the occasion".

George White, the Mayor of Tenby, presided as numerous toasts and speeches were made, the breezy utterances of David Davies evidently doing the most to entertain. Replying to a toast to the contractors he observed that "I could not see any reason for an outlay of capital until I came back to Tenby and saw the ladies, and I was at once convinced . . ." He knew, he said, "that where such ladies were the gentlemen would soon follow!"

Initially the railway provided three trains a day each way, and although the number was increased to five each way by September, the service was cut back to three in December, 1863. The fares between the two towns were 2/- (10p) return first class and 1/6 (7½p) return second class; fares to and from Manorbier were at half these prices. By the end of 1863 it was reckoned that the railway had already carried 40,000 passengers, and a coach service was operating between Pembroke and Hobbs Point pier. There were no Sunday trains because the contractors were convinced Methodists and refused to disrupt the day of rest. Some shareholders disliked this policy but they had to admit that the contractors were good workers, and their progress "very satisfactory".

According to an Engineer's report made on 18th August, 1863, opening of the line west of Pembroke was dependent largely on the completion of the cutting at Golden Hill, and this was receiving attention. However, the embankment over the Mill Pond at Pembroke had been carried over the culvert, and the driftway in the tunnel near Golden Hill was progressing steadily, about a quarter of the whole length having been driven from each end. In the meantime some citizens of Pembroke did not show wholehearted gratitude for their new means of transport: complaints were made that the station was too far out of town. David Davies suggested that another station should be built near Golden Hill. This idea was not taken up, but the contractors did make alterations to two overbridges near Pembroke which traders claimed were too narrow for their carts. Further west, at Pembroke Dock, there was difficulty over the site for the railway's terminus. Owing to delays in the acquisition of government land at Hobbs Point it was not possible to lay rails right through to the pier. Pending the grant of Parliamentary powers to build a permanent terminus at Dimond Street it was decided to provide a temporary station some fourteen chains further east at the nearest point on the authorised route to Hobbs Point.

Davies & Roberts had contracted to complete the line within two years, and having finished the greater part of it within one year they wasted no time in tackling the rest. The tunnel was driven through on the last day of 1863, and Ezra Roberts was the first man to step through. On 18th February, 1864, James Mathias reported this to shareholders and said that:

> . . . since then the rails have been laid through to admit the passage of large earth wagons and the opening out for the masonry has been commenced in three places equidistant from each other . . . The whole should be completed in May so that allowing for unforeseen hindrances I confidently expect the remaining portion of your railway to be open to the public in the month of June.

The Engineer's estimate was not far out: after inspection by the Board of Trade the railway was declared ready for opening on 9th August, 1864.

On the opening day business was suspended in Pembroke Dock, and bunting and banners put up, including some proclaiming "Success to the Railway and trade of Pembroke Dock". At the temporary station a vast crowd gathered. After heavy rain up to 11 o'clock the day became beautifully fine, and in due course the opening train arrived, decked with garlands and banners. Consisting of every carriage the company possessed — fifteen in all, in addition to vans — it was crammed with passengers. A great cheer went up as the train rolled in, and the passengers responded loudly. A procession was promptly formed at the station, and the dignitaries and others were then lead through the streets by "an excellent band". At the Victoria Hotel Jonas Dawkins, Mayor of Pembroke, presided over a banquet for two hundred guests, amongst whom was Richard Potter, Chairman of the Great Western Railway. Following the GW's complete take over of the South Wales Railway in 1863 Potter had reason to be interested in the occasion, even though the P&T was not a broad gauge line. He was probably even more interested in the development of Milford Haven, because two days later his wife laid the foundation stone for new docks at Milford. On that occasion he expressed reservations about the development of Milford and Neyland and Pembroke Dock. At the banquet at Pembroke Dock, however, his caution did nothing to mar the occasion. After many speeches and toasts the celebrations were brought to a close in the evening by a grand firework display. Davies & Roberts were the heroes of the day. They had fulfilled their bargain and the line was open throughout.

Chapter Four
The Whitland Extension

Whilst the line to Pembroke Dock was under construction plans were going ahead for the extension of the P&TR to Whitland. There was more to this than the simple desire to make a link with the South Wales main line, and to put this in perspective a brief account of some neighbouring lines is necessary. Fourteen miles east of Whitland, at Carmarthen, a local company had been struggling to build a broad gauge railway north towards Newcastle Emlyn and Cardigan. Authorised in 1854 as the Carmarthen & Cardigan Railway, persistent financial difficulties prevented the line being opened to Pencader and Llandyssul until 1864. Newcastle Emlyn was not reached until 1895 (by which time the C&CR was Great Western property) and the line was never extended beyond.

Much further north, in Lancashire, Manchester businessmen dreamt of side-stepping Liverpool's dominance over local trade. As early as the 1840s there was a scheme to join Manchester and Milford Haven by a railway through the Welsh Hills. That project fell through, but the dream did not die. Milford Haven was widely seen as a harbour with a future, a port for America as well as Ireland. By 1862 standard gauge rails stretched from Manchester to Llanidloes in mid-Wales, and broad gauge track reached from New Milford to Carmarthen. All that was needed for the direct route was a line between Llanidloes and the ailing C&CR. This was authorised by the Manchester & Milford Railway Act of 1860.

Like the Pembroke & Tenby Railway, the Manchester & Milford soon found it difficult to transfer its plans from paper onto the ground, and for a while little progress was made. In 1863 a wealthy industrialist named John Barrow joined the M&M board, and the company's fortunes took a turn for the better. David Davies was consulted, and in February 1864 he and Frederick Beeston became contractors to the company. Construction began, and enthusiasm for the M&MR flourished. Closer to the sheltered waters of Milford Haven, the P&T's Directors became increasingly keen to link up with the M&M and other standard gauge lines to the North and Midlands. The snag for the P&T was the stretch of broad gauge track west and north of Carmarthen: without a through standard gauge line they faced the expense and inconvenience of trans-shipment of goods wherever the gauged met. Nothing daunted, in 1863 the P&T, after contemplating an extension to Narberth Road, decided to seek powers to build a railway between Tenby and Whitland.

At this stage the supporters of the abortive Whitland & Milford Haven Railway were still not convinced of the merits of the P&T, in spite of Davies & Roberts' good work. By the spring of 1863 they had

PROPOSED RAILWAYS EAST OF WHITLAND

(Omitting the Whitland, Cronware & Pendine Railway, authorised in 1877 but not built)

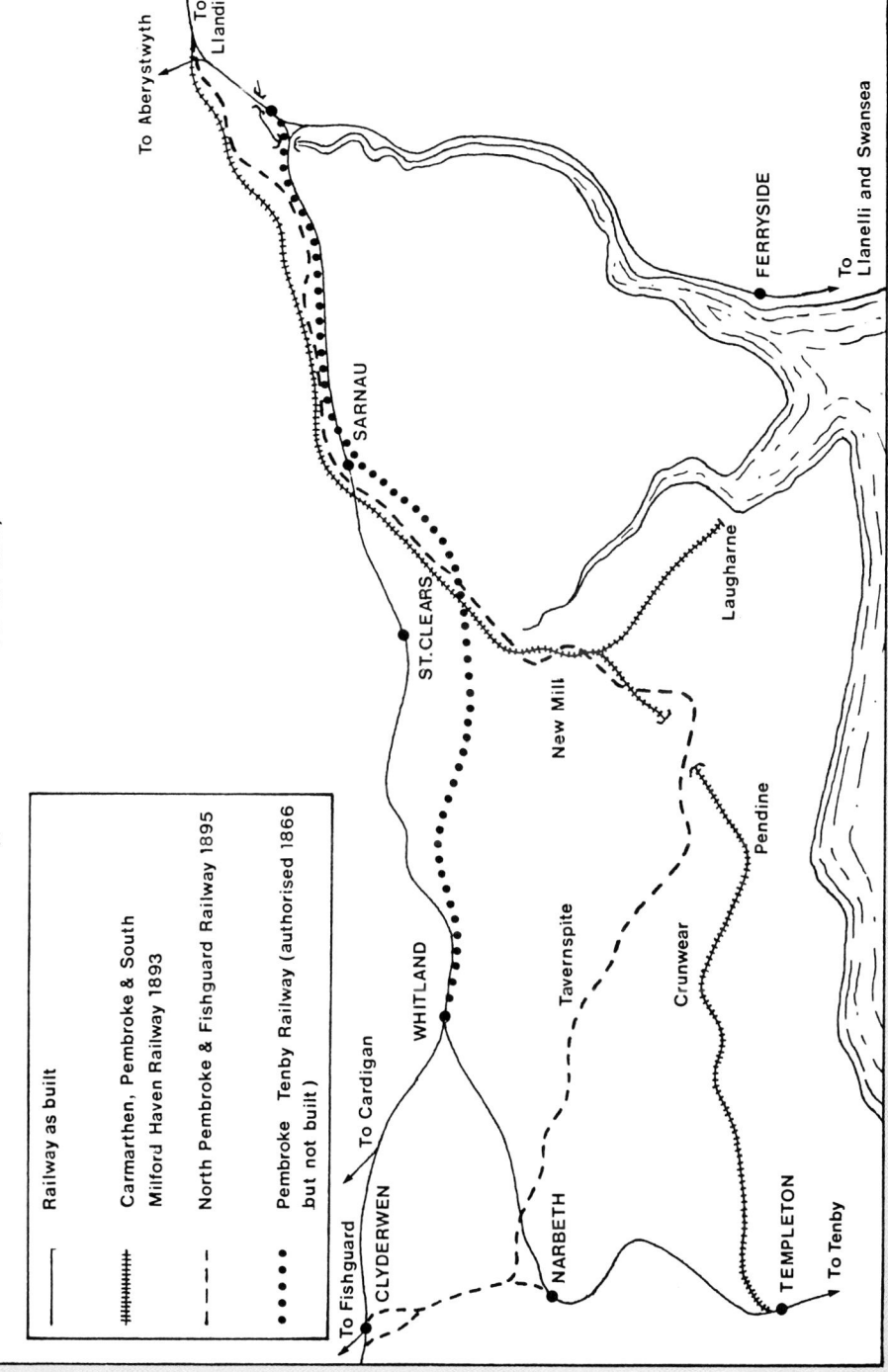

discussed their scheme with the contractors Messrs Brassey & Field. For some time they remained unreconciled to the P&TR, apparently inspiring another rival entitled the South Wales, Tenby and Milford Haven Junction Railway. A Parliamentary Bill for this 4' 8½" gauge line was prepared for the 1863/64 session, but never formally presented. According to plans prepared by the engineers C.B. Lane and Edward Bagot, the scheme envisaged a railway 14 miles 6 furlongs 1 chain in length, from the SWR to Tenby, taking the approximate route of the Saundersfoot Railway between Stepaside and Saundersfoot Harbour, before running on round and through the cliffs to Tenby to make an end-on junction with the new P&TR. Shades of the South Devon Railway near Dawlish! Suffice to say, though, that as the P&T's own Bill made progress, this project fizzled out. In due course C.R. Vickerman of Saundersfoot actually gave evidence for the P&T's Bill; significantly, perhaps, it provided for a direct connection between the P&T and the Saundersfoot Railway.

The Pembroke & Tenby Railway Act, 1864 (as the Bill became) authorised several new sections of railway, of which only the first two formed the extension between Tenby and Whitland. The third section reflected the P&T's desire to link up with other 4' 8½" gauge lines by providing for a 52½ chain loop at Carmarthen between the C&CR and the GWR, facing Whitland. It also reflected the rather large assumption that both the GWR and the C&CR would accommodate the P&T's standard gauge track. The other sections of line were designed to tap the coalfield, one being a spur of only three furlongs curving north west from Saundersfoot to the Saundersfoot Railway, and the other a westward extension of the same line to serve collieries at Broadmoor. The Act, which authorised capital of £200,000 in shares and £66,600 in loans, also provided for the company to purchase extra land at Pembroke Dock for the construction of a permanent station.

As soon as the railway was open to Pembroke Dock, the contractors concentrated their attention upon the Whitland extension. On 17th August, 1864, it was reported that their men had started to clear trees on Tenby Green, near the P&T station. Even so, the £200,000 contract for the building of the extension was not signed until 3rd October. This included terms for the work to be completed within two years, and for payment to be made largely in preference shares. Arrangements for the purchase of the necessary land went ahead promptly, and by 8th February, 1865, the Engineer was able to state that the route had been set out and full plans prepared for the extension as far as Narberth station. Work was progressing on the first mile, and "next week" the contractors were expected to gain possession of another two miles and begin making several cuttings.

In the following week the Engineer thought that work on the

cutting at Cold Blow, near Narberth, might be possible. As construction continued swiftly during 1865 and 1866 large sums were paid to Davies & Roberts in respect of work done. Between April and September, 1865, for example, over £80,000 was paid to the contractors, mostly in shares.

Davies & Roberts' involvement with the P&T was not confined to the task of construction. By a series of agreements they also undertook to work the line. The first was made on 18th July, 1863, in time for the opening of the railway twelve days later. The contractors appear to have assumed responsibility for the provision of locomotives and rolling stock, as well as the running of trains. To deal with the administration of their service it is almost certain that they (rather than the company) appointed the Traffic Manager, a young Cardiganshire man named Isaac Smedley. Next, on 8th August, 1864, the contractors entered into what was virtually a lease of the P&TR. They agreed to work the Pembroke Dock–Tenby section for five years from 1st July, 1864, receiving all the proceeds but paying existing shareholders 5% on the amount of their shares. The agreement soon ran into difficulties. On 25th August the P&T Board was advised that it had no power to grant a lease for working the line for a term of years, and so withdrew its approval to the agreemnet of 8th August. Instead it resolved simply to accept the offer of Davies & Roberts "to work the line, receive proceeds and pay 5% to shareholders". Operations continued on this open-ended basis until 13th February, 1867, when, following the completion of the Whitland extension, the company approved a new agreement with the contractors for working the line between Pembroke Dock and Whitland.

On occasions Davies & Roberts' complete dominance of the company's business appears to have been an embarrassment. When the P&T's 1864 Bill was being considered by the Select Committee of the House of Commons, James Mathias was questioned about the contractors. As they had provided all but £5000 of the capital their shareholding was huge, and evidently so large as to be of doubtful legality. Under pressure the Engineer reluctantly acknowledged that Davies & Roberts held ⁷/₁₀ths of the shares. The actual figure seems to have been about ⅝ths. Two years later, when George Mathias was giving evidence to the Select Committee on the P&T's next Bill, he stated that David Davies "held a considerable amount of shares — about or more than one third". Even allowing for Roberts' holding this was probably an under estimate. At this period the Pembroke & Tenby was, for most practical purposes, Davies & Roberts' railway.

Although Ezra Roberts was David Davies' partner, he is a curiously shadowy figure. Prior to 1868 he is mentioned on numerous occasions, but later he is hardly referred to at all. From start to finish

David Davies got most of the glory, and not only with the public at large. Davies respected his workmen, and had their loyalty and affection in return. As a keen Methodist he held himself morally responsible for their spiritual welfare. Many were Welsh Calvinistic Methodists, and in the absence of any chapel of this description David Davies built one for their use at Nestor Square, Narberth. In addition preachers were invited to speak to the men in barns or other suitable buildings near the site of the works, and at least one scholarly minister, named Charles Edwards, was a successful pastor as well as preacher amongst the navvies.

For David Davies this was a period of transition, marking the last phase of his career as a railway contractor and the first of his career as a coal owner and politician. In 1864 he and several others (including Ezra Roberts) leased mineral rights in a tract of land at Treorchy in the Rhondda Valley. After fifteen months searching for coal the sheer expense brought Davies to the point of giving up; his loyal workmen decided to work one last week for nothing, and on Friday 9th March, 1866, they struck coal. According to his biographer Ivor Thomas, Davies was then supervising work on the Whitland extension. When he got news of the find at Treorchy he brandished the telegram before his foreman, William Thomas, and declared "It's all right, I would not take £40,000 for this piece of paper. They have struck the seam at Cwmparc!" All in all Davies had something to celebrate that month, because the rails were laid from Tenby almost to Templeton, and work on the rest of the extension was well advanced. Within another two months the railway was complete to a point near Narberth tunnel, and it was possible for the contractors' locomotive to make a trial trip, watched by many fascinated spectators.

As will shortly be seen, in the summer of 1866 the P&TR obtained powers to extend their line to Carmarthen. With the Whitland extension nearing completion, the Manchester & Milford dream seemed much closer to becoming reality. Congratulating shareholders on the P&T's progress, William Owen spoke optimistically to a half yearly meeting on 29th August: "I hope by June next year you will see a direct line through to Manchester and the North. It is what we have been fighting for for many years, and now we see the last link almost completed". At the same meeting William Owen recalled that when the P&T was started it was said it would be very little good to the country and would not pay. Refuting the critics he pointed out that, whereas in the year ending June 1864, 101,452 passengers had passed over the line, in the year ending June 1865, the total had been 143,145. Furthermore, the growth had continued, and in the half-year ending June 1866, passengers increased by 10,300 over the corresponding half year of 1865. With some pride Owen observed "You may see what this little line has done, and the accommodation it gives." He concluded by asking shareholders to accept a 5% dividend on shares, in accordance with the arrangement with Davies & Roberts.

The Whitland extension was now finished, and the Board of Trade inspection took place on 1st September, 1866. That day, according to David Davies, he asked the Inspector, Captain Rich, if he had ever heard of sixteen miles of railway being completed so rapidly. He replied, "Never". Later Davies commented that it could not have been done if he had not had money and "stood upon the works day after day, night after night, to say how they were progressing." No wonder Davies' enjoyed his workmen's trust! At any rate, as Captain Rich regarded the construction of the railway as entirely satisfactory, the Whitland extension was opened for public traffic on Tuesday 4th September, 1866. Stations were provided at Saundersfoot, Kilgetty and Narberth, in addition to the terminus adjacent to the GWR at Whitland. To judge from one contemporary report trains also stopped at Templeton, on the opening day at least even though the station was not completed until 1867. A new station was also provided at Tenby for Pembroke Dock–Whitland through trains; as some of the works were unfinished it seems that the original station did not close to passengers at once.

The day after the opening of the Whitland extension, the *Haverfordwest & Milford Haven Telegraph* reported the event with typical enthusiasm: "The contractors . . . have constructed a railway as it were in a night — a railway which will by the early part of next year, when the Great Western Railway Company have fulfilled their compact, connect the world-renowned Milford Haven by a narrow gauge line with Manchester and the North of England". Of the compact more must be said, but after noting that "the out-door demonstrations in connection with the opening ceremony were of a much less imposing nature than might otherwise have been expected," the paper recorded that in the afternoon a grand banquet had been held at the Cobourg Hotel, Tenby. This had been a great success, the contractors receiving addresses from their workmen and from the Mayor, Aldermen and Burgesses of Tenby. David Davies used the occasion to speak with refreshing frankness! "I do not wish any misunderstanding to exist about the history of the Pembroke & Tenby Railway . . . My partner and I went into the matter as a pure speculation for the sake of profit — whereas the gentlemen of the directorate have done what they have done for no motive save the good of the district." Although he was ready to leave the honour of the Directors, honour was rightly given to Messrs Davies & Roberts. They had made the railway a reality, and once again were the heroes of the hour. The Whitland Extension seems to have met with prompt approval. In the first half of 1867 (it is said) the railway carried 91,849 passengers and conveyed 250 tons limestone per day on average. On the opening of the Whitland extension trains began to run "up" to Whitland rather than "up" to Pembroke Dock.

TOURIST TICKETS

Available for Two Calendar Months,

TO

SOUTH WALES.

FARES FOR THE DOUBLE JOURNEY.

FROM	Carmarthen.			Tenby, via Whitland.			Pembroke and Pembroke Dock, via Whitland.			Swansea.		
	1st cl.	2nd cl.	3rd cl.	1st cl.	2nd cl.	3rd cl.	1st cl.	2nd cl.	3rd cl.	1st cl.	2nd cl.	3rd cl.
	s. d.	s. d.	s. d.	s. d.	s. d.	s. d.	s. d.	s. d.	s. d.	s. d.	s. d.	s. d.
Whitchurch ...	40 6	29 9	18 0	50 9	37 3	23 0	50 9	37 3	23 0	...	...	...
Ellesmere	40 6	29 9	18 0	50 9	37 3	21 0	50 9	37 3	21 0	...	...	...
Oswestry	40 6	29 9	17 0	50 9	37 3	20 6	48 0	35 0	20 6	36 3	26 0	17 0
Llanymynech	39 0	28 6	17 0	50 9	37 3	20 6	48 0	35 0	20 6	...	...	...
Welshpool......	35 6	25 6	17 0	45 9	33 0	20 6	48 0	35 0	20 6	...	...	...
Newtown	35 6	25 6	17 0	47 6	32 6	20 0	50 0	34 6	20 0	...	...	...
Llanidloes......	35 6	25 6	17 0	48 6	33 6	20 0	51 0	35 6	20 0	...	...	...
Machynlleth..	...	...	...	38 0	26 0	15 6	40 6	28 0	17 0	...	...	...
Portmadoc ...	...	...	...	51 0	35 0	21 0	53 6	37 0	23 0	...	...	...
Pwllheli	...	...	...	55 0	38 0	23 0	57 6	40 0	24 6	...	...	...

These Tickets are available via Aberystwith and Manchester and Milford Railway, or via Llanidloes, Builth Road, and Llandilo, or via Llanidloes and Neath (except those for Swansea, which are available via Llanidloes, Builth Road, and Llandovery, or via Llanidloes, Brecon, and Midland Railway.)

Passengers must state at the time of booking which route they intend to travel, and take tickets accordingly.

Passengers for Carmarthen, Tenby, Pembroke, and Pembroke Dock, travelling via Aberystwith, can break their journey at Aberystwith or Carmarthen, those travelling via Llanidloes, Builth Road, and Llandilo, at Rhayader and Llandovery, and those travelling via Llanidloes and Neath at Brecon and Neath.

Passengers for Swansea can break their journey at Llanidloes, Rhayader, and Brecon.

First and Third Class Tickets only are issued by the Midland route.

A 1904 Cambrian Railway Timetable extract.

Chapter Five
The P & T at Carmarthen

Whilst the Whitland extension was being built, the dream of linking the P&T line with other standard gauge railways was not forgotten for a moment. Initially the company had thought in terms of persuading the Great Western to lay mixed gauge track on its line between Whitland and Carmarthen, granting the P&T running powers over the section. It soon became obvious that the GWR would not co-operate. On 12th October, 1865, the P&T Board resolved that "all attempts at a compromise with the GWR Co. having failed the company engineer Mr James Mathias be instructed to survey an independent line from Whitland to Carmarthen . . ." No doubt with the difficulties of August 1864 in mind the Board also decided to seek powers to enable the company "to grant a lease for a term of years to parties for working the line". Preparations were made quickly, and by 11th December the Board was studying a draft of a Parliamentary Bill for the extension from Whitland to Carmarthen.

The estimated cost of all the works contemplated by the Bill was £157,000. The Hobbs Point line and works at Pembroke accounted for £54,000, whilst the Whitland–Carmarthen single line accounted for £103,000. As surveyed this route was 14 miles 16 chains long, and ran south of the existing line for several miles before passing close to the village of St Clears. It crossed the GWR near the site of the later station of Sarnau, and was then aligned almost alongside the Great Western into Carmarthen. The scheme envisaged the building of the P&T spur at Carmarthen, authorised in 1864, and according to the plans this single line was to join the C&CR just south of their bridge over the River Towy. At the far end of the bridge the line ran into Carmarthen Town, a station which at this date consisted of little more than a loop with platforms on each side. The main building was on the down side, and a goods shed stood to the north of it.

In spite of Great Western opposition the Bill was passed in 1866. The Act authorised the P&T to raise an additional £115,000 in shares and £38,000 in loans, although by 1870 only £20,000 in debentures had been issued in respect of the Carmarthen extension. The P&T rightly anticipated that once it had powers for a line to Carmarthen the GWR would be willing to negotiate. As William Owen said "as we thought there was no need to make another line to run parallel with theirs, and they were disposed to come to terms, we arranged with the Great Western for laying down a narrow gauge from Whitland to Carmarthen". Although briefly put, there was more to it than that, because by now Davies and Beeston's work on the Manchester & Milford Railway was progressing well. For the P&T, making a connection with the M&M was a matter of immediate interest, especially as the first section between Pencader and Lampeter was nearly ready for freight, and the M&M was about to gain access to Carmarthen over mixed gauge track south of Pencader.

Agreement between the P&T and the Great Western was reached rapidly. On 18th July, 1866, the latter agreed to convert its up line from Whitland to Carmarthen to the 4' 8½" gauge to enable P&T trains to reach Carmarthen Town via the proposed P&T loop. In return the P&T agreed not to build its recently authorised extension, and to contribute £20,000 towards the costs of the up line conversion. For the Great Western this was no bad deal, because it was already under pressure from shareholders and businessmen to convert all its South Wales lines to the narrower gauge. Indeed, in terms of railway politics it was a master stroke, because by accommodating the standard gauge on its own property the GWR kept a grip on all rail traffic in and out of Pembrokeshire. Already the powerful London & North Western Railway was showing interest in the P&T as it extended its influence westwards with the construction of the standard gauge Central Wales Railway; had the P&T reached Carmarthen by its own route subsequent history might well have been different. In the event the main legacy of the P&T's Carmarthen extension plan was a dispute between James Mathias and the company over the costs of his survey. Although a settlement was reached in July 1868, the rift was deep, and by then the Engineer had ended his association with the company.

The GWR's tactics were as skilful as their strategy. Having reached an agreement with the P&T they dragged their feet over its implementation. The delay deferred P&T competition at Carmarthen, and denied the company traffic. The P&T was frustrated, but eventually, in November 1867, issued formal notice requiring the GWR to comply with their agreement. Difficulties continued to arise. The P&T wanted to see mixed gauge track on both the up and down lines east of Whitland, and asserted that a much smaller sum than £20,000 "would have sufficed had the agreement been only to alter one line". However, David Davies was allowed to conduct negotiations, and on 14th May, 1868 he accepted the arrangements for the conversion of the up line only. At the same time or earlier the company also agreed to payment for the use of the converted track; this is believed to have been £4,500 per annum. In winning such terms the GWR undoubtedly made good use of its muscle; in accepting them Davies was probably being realistic.

The up line between Whitland and Carmarthen was the first portion of Brunel's broad gauge to be converted to the standard gauge. Track of each gauge was laid side by side on the same track bed, and the gauges were mixed only at the intermediate station of St

Clears, to enable trains to pass. In addition a loop was provided on the narrow gauge at Carmarthen Bridge to minimise shunting at Carmarthen. Although it has often been said that there was no problem in singling the broad gauge because traffic was light Sir O.H.P. Scourfield recalled years later that the arrangement caused the GWR great inconvenience. Suffice to say the conversion work was completed by 1st June, 1868, and the first P&T train that day is said to have taken a consignment of lime from Tenby to Carmarthen Town. At the outset there was no P&T passenger service east of Whitland, but at the half-yearly meeting held on 24th August, 1868, the Directors congratulated the shareholders on the extension of the line to Carmarthen. They also declared that the railway's revenue "continued most satisfactory", showing an increase of £1351 on the corresponding six months of the previous year.

The Carmarthen extension soon proved to be a better proposition on paper than it was in fact. Quite apart from the P&T's uneasy relationship with the Great Western, the company had to contend with the conflicting aspirations of three other concerns — the M&MR, the C&CR, and the Llanelly Railway, owners of the line from Llandilo to Carmarthen (opened to goods in 1844 and to passengers on 1st June, 1865). The P&T was bound by Act of Parliament to work traffic from the M&M and Llanelly railways, and to take through carriages, but the C&CR at Carmarthen insisted on a four mile clause for through traffic. This provided that a fare for four miles should be paid on any journey of less, but as the P&T operated over only 48 chains of the Cardigan line, they felt this stipulation was harsh. To make matters worse the P&T apparently had already agreed to pay £350 p.a. rent for the use of Carmarthen Town — a station on a marsh some distance from the town centre, and at this time lacking proper road access!

This situation contained all the ingredients for argument. In the autumn of 1868 the Llanelly company asked the P&TR to book passengers for its line; Mr Smedley replied by saying the P&T would be happy to do so as soon as their own passenger service was extended to Carmarthen. The Llanelly company was not pleased and by January 1869 it had a Bill before Parliament seeking (*inter alia*) running powers over the P&TR. The P&T petitioned against this and, although the Llanelly railway obtained powers over the C&CR from Abergwili Junction to Carmarthen Town, they did not win powers over the P&T.

A more dramatic row developed between the P&T and the C&CR. The former exercised its running powers partly to run lime traffic through to Carmarthen for forward movement to the M&MR, and partly to exchange traffic with the Llanelly Railway. The C&C soon felt that the Pembroke company was not paying a full rent for the use of its metals. The P&T argued otherwise, but for at least three days in May 1869, the C&C obstructed through traffic. The P&T and Llanelly companies promptly employed horse drawn carts to take goods between the P&T south of Carmarthen Town and the Llanelly Railway to the north of it.

One consignment — four wagons of iron plates to Pembroke Dock — was so urgent that it was sent back from Carmarthen to Llanelly on the standard gauge, transferred to the broad gauge, and turned over to the standard gauge again at Whitland! Although the obstruction was lifted the trouble was not over, because it seems that the C&C stopped traffic on other occasions soon after. However, further negotiations took place on the use of Carmarthen Town, and on 23rd July, 1869, the P&T and C&C reached an agreement which opened the door to a P&T passenger service to Carmarthen.

The service duly started at the beginning of August 1869. G.P. Neale, well known as superintendent of the line LNWR, records that shortly after the P&T passenger service reached Carmarthen, Tenby had the advantage of through trains for the first time. The through trains were in fact through coaches from Liverpool and Manchester via the LNWR's Central Wales route — a route which in spite of the M&M's ambitions was already on its way to becoming the nearest thing to a trunk line between Manchester and Milford Haven. The GWR was alive to the implications of the development, and being anxious to avoid flirtation between the standard gauge companies, gave further thought to abandoning the broad gauge in South Wales. Financial constraints deferred this decision until February 1871. Fifteen months later, on Saturday 11th May, 1872, the decision was put into effect. The last broad gauge working through Whitland was, appropriately enough, the 2–4–0 named *Brunel* running light engine from New Milford. The gauge conversion took place immediately, and, somewhat cheekily, the Great Western asked the P&T to contribute towards the cost. The P&T was understandably reluctant but, perhaps for diplomatic reasons, eventually provided rails from sidings at Lamphey and Whitland to enable a section of double track to be laid at the junction at Carmarthen.

With the conversion of the broad gauge the struggle between the companies came to a head. In May 1872, the LNWR timetable announced the running of through coaches to Tenby from Euston, as well as Manchester, Crewe and Shrewsbury. The GWR promptly arranged through carriages from Paddington to Pembroke Dock. Although this service ran via Gloucester, it must be wondered how many then troubled to take the much longer route from Euston via Stafford and Shrewsbury! The P&T collaborated as best it could with both sides. Years later G.P. Neale observed that "Mr Smedley, the

Manager of the Pembroke & Tenby line, had his difficulties in keeping on friendly terms with his broad gauge neighbours and his narrow gauge allies". This was fair comment, and never more so than in the summer of 1872 when the broad gauge came to an end in South Wales.

Despite the LNWR's desire to gain influence in west Wales, the Great Western had little to worry about: narrowing the gauge was the key to securing its position in Pembrokeshire. Arrangements with the P&T were re-negotiated, and a new agreement was concluded on 31st July, 1872. By it the GWR conceded that the P&T contributed to its traffic, and agreed to pay year by year 5% of the increased proportion of revenue over the value of traffic exchanged in the year ending 31st July, 1872. The terms do not appear to have been generous to the P&T, which had a high price to pay in other ways. On 1st August, 1872, all P&T passenger services east of Whitland came to an end, and the P&T loop at Carmarthen was reduced to siding status. Instead through carriages were attached to Great Western trains stopping at Carmarthen Junction, from which point they could be detached and worked through to Carmarthen Town. Although even the P&T's weekday freight service ran direct to Carmarthen Junction, for some while the company had hopes of re-opening the loop: six years later orders were given for the loop signal box to be repainted. However it was a sign of the times (and the effectiveness of Great Western diplomacy) that on 1st July, 1872 C&CR through rates to the P&T were withdrawn. By a separate agreement the M&M on 1st August ceased to run over the C&C into Carmarthen Town, and terminated its trains at Pencader. Not surprisingly, after the summer of 1872 no more was heard of LNWR through coaches from Euston!

In retrospect these agreements of 31st July, 1872, can be seen as natural successors to the agreement of 18th July, 1866. Together they isolated the P&T from its standard gauge friends, and blocked any ideas those companies might have had for venturing further into west Wales. Even so, an ambitious LNWR never lost hope of gaining ground. Late in 1872 two companies under its influence, the Llanelly Railway and the Swansea & Carmarthen Railway (formed in 1871, and including the Llanelly's Llandilo–Carmarthen line) tried to win running powers over the P&T. The GWR objected and encouraged the P&T to do the same. In the face of opposition the Llanelly withdrew, but the Swansea and Carmarthen persisted. They made no progress; Mr Grierson of the GWR later sent a £400 donation towards P&T expenses as the Great Western appreciated "the able and vigorous manner in which your company opposed the Bill". Typically the contribution was smaller than the P&T expected: at the time the GW was not the P&T's most popular neighbour!

Chapter Six
The New Men

The Pembroke & Tenby Railway was without an official Engineer for several months after the departure of James Mathias. In the interim the company must have relied upon the competence of the contractors, and Isaac Smedley, who seems to have had day to day responsibility for locomotives. In January 1869 however, the Board appointed James W. Szlumper as Engineer, at a salary of £88 per annum. Szlumper had been Engineer of the Manchester & Milford Railway for several years, and his appointment on the P&T may well have owed something to David Davies, contractor to both companies. At any rate, Szlumper took up his duties promptly and a month later made the customary Engineer's report to the half-year meeting of shareholders. Having assured them that the permanent way, bridges and rolling stock were in satisfactory repair, he made reference to the standard gauge Whitland & Taf Vale Railway which had just been given Parliamentary approval. The W&TV, he said, "cannot fail to be a valuable feeder to your railway as opening out a district in which a large traffic in lime, slates and lead and other minerals will be developed". The fact that William Owen and David Davies were Directors of the W&TV no doubt influenced Szlumper's sentiments. However, he was not impartial himself, because he became Engineer to the P&T shortly after appointment to a similar post on the W&TV. By 1869 Szlumper was Engineer to no less than three west Wales railways!

David Davies and James Szlumper worked together on numerous occasions from the building of the M&M in the 1860s, to the construction of the Barry Railway and docks in the 1880s. In the early years, at least, their railway interests enjoyed the fortunate financial backing of the Barrows, a family with roots in Nottinghamshire and Derbyshire. Exactly why the family became so involved in Welsh schemes is not certain, but in the early 1860s John Barrow seems to have been impressed by the dream of a great Manchester to Milford trunk railway. Plainly he had the Victorian's willingness to take commercial risks: already he had had a successful career as a businessman and banker in London. His brother Richard was of a similar stamp, inspiring the development of the Staveley iron and coal works in Derbyshire. In an age which rewarded enterprise, their efforts had won them immense wealth. Now their prosperity became a blessing for both the M&M and the P&T lines.

In the summer of 1869 John Barrow, his son John James Barrow, and an associate George Edward Forster joined the Board of the P&T. The available papers say virtually nothing about the events leading up to their appointment, but the main factor must have been their money. Indeed, it can hardly be a coincidence that after the Barrows arrived there is no reference to Ezra Roberts. As the contractors were by far the largest shareholders the conclusion must be that the Barrows bought up a considerable quantity of the contractors' holding. Already John Barrow had taken over a large slice of Davies' interest in the M&M, and during 1869 he bought £2000 worth of shares in the infant W&TV. John Barrow obviously wanted to get involved in west Wales. David Davies must have been glad to encourage him: by now he was deeply committed to Rhondda coal mining, and had every reason to want to realise some of his capital. In effect, therefore, Davies & Roberts sold to the Barrows the control of the P&TR.

The surviving P&T papers make no clear reference to the Barrows and Forster before November 1869, by which time company administration was being divided between a Pembroke Dock committee and a London committee. The former, comprising local Directors, was established in August, 1869. The latter was not formally constituted until February 1870, but as it consisted of the Barrows and Forster it was active informally much earlier. Whilst the Pembroke Dock committee was preoccupied with plans for a government telegraph along the line (completed in June 1870) the London committee was dealing with the Parliamentary proceedings for the P&T's 1870 Act for the Dockyard extension line. There can be little doubt which was the dominant committee: plainly power had passed to London.

By the time the London committee met on 13th April, 1870, they had studied the several contracts between the contractors and the company, and the contractors were preparing to hand over the working of the P&T with effect from 1st July. As Davies & Roberts no longer held a majority shareholding this step was logical enough. Between April and July, however, negotiations continued on the construction contracts to assess what was still to be done on each side. David Davies undertook to complete within six months all works outstanding under the agreements of 4th August, 1862 and 3rd October, 1864. The company for its part agreed to pay Davies £15,000, in shares, out of a total of £28,782 still due to him. Just to complicate matters the company's solicitor later expressed the opinion that this issue of shares to him might be illegal!

30th June, 1870, marked the end of an era on the Pembroke & Tenby Railway: after seven years it ceased to be a contractors' railway. An impression of the state of the line at this time is provided by the Report and Statement of Accounts for the first half of 1870. After reporting the passing of the 1870 Act this revealed that revenue for the half year totalled £11,121 2s. 8d., an increase of £371 over the comparable half year of 1869. Passenger receipts in the period amounted to £4779 3s. 0d., and the ticket returns indicated that about 86% travelled 3rd class, 10% 2nd class and 4% 1st class. Mineral traffic produced £4232 and general merchandise £1517. Receipts from livestock, mails and other sources were comparatively insignificant. The net revenue after payment of operating expenses, interest charges, rents and rates was no less than £6028 — enabling the agreed 5% dividend to be paid. Under Davies & Roberts the P&T was paying its way! It is more sobering to record that the total bill for wages and salaries on a railway of which 27 miles 34 chains were maintained, and 41 miles 12 chains were worked, was £2033 2s. 6d. As the contractors were in charge, though, it is not clear what payments (if any) they made to operating staff. Passenger and mail train mileage totalled 37,467 (about 3000 miles more than in the first half of 1869) and goods and mineral train mileage 16,437 (about 5000 miles down compared with 1869). The Report and Accounts were signed by William Owen as Chairman, and Isaac Smedley, who was described as company accountant as well as Manager. The company's offices were at Pembroke Dock, and the Secretary was Thomas Stokes. In addition to Owen, the Directors were John Barrow, John James Barrow, Stephen Robinson, F.L. Clark and G.E. Forster. Only Owen and Clark lived in Pembrokeshire, and for practical purposes constituted the Pembroke Dock committee.

The first half year of P&T working was quite successful: at the end of it the company declared a dividend of 5% on Preference shares and 1% on Ordinary shares. During these months, however, the Directors were taking stock of the situation. The question of Davies & Roberts' construction contracts was submitted to arbitration, and the eventual outcome appears to have been complex. Various financial and shareholding adjustments were recommended, and in addition it was thought that Davies had some liability in respect of the unbuilt Hobbs Point branch, and responsibility for completing a station at Tenby to the value of £600, and a goods shed of £300. A station to be finished at Pembroke Dock was to cost £500. Subject to the details of the arbitrators' award, and the completion of these buildings, the Board agreed that the existing contracts had been satisfied. Even so, it must be evidence of good relations that on 31st August, 1870, the company decided to enter into a new contract with Davies, for the building of the recently authorised Dockyard Extension line. Over a year later, after Davies had started work on the Hobbs Point branch, the company also signed a new contract for its construction.

Although Isaac Smedley was a protégé of the contractors, he was asked to continue as manager. Indeed his influence seems to have increased, because he now gained direct responsibility for locomotives and rolling stock. Before long he negotiated the hire of thirty wagons from the Bristol Wagon Co. and in 1871 he took a central role in seeking more motive power for the railway. In the meantime he made arrangements for the P&T to have its own telegraph between Whitland and Tenby, evidently quite apart from the government telegraph to Pembroke Dock. He was also an advocate of a regular mail service on the P&T, and soon proposed the running of Sunday trains. These were instituted in the summer months of 1871. Fares, salaries, uniforms, materials, building alterations and insurance — Isaac Smedley was given charge of them all. Whatever the problem Smedley seems to have been competent to tackle it, retaining authority and respect even in the thorny issues of personnel management. He sought the Directors' advice on applications for wage increases, or cuts in working hours, and often could not give what was wanted. When appropriate he used his initiative: a memorable minute of 4th August, 1871 records the verdict on one of his proposals: "it was agreed that boys should not be used as heretofore in watching the cornfields along the line to prevent any ignition caused by the engines, the risk of damage being taken by the company for this present summer." In short, another relic of the Davies & Roberts era was ended.

In the summer of 1871 John Barrow died, and at the same time William Owen retired from the Board. He appears to have taken no active part in the company thereafter. On 31st August, 1871, John James Barrow was elected Chairman on the proposal of S. Robinson. A few days later, on 7th September he was also elected to the Board of the Whitland & Taf Vale Railway, then under construction. Evidently he had a reason for such involvement: informal discussions ensued on the possibility of the P&TR working the W&TVR. Less than a year later, on 24th May, 1872, J.J. Barrow resigned from the W&TV Board. Subsequently the Chairman of the latter company stated that it had been found impossible to place certain shares "except under the condition of handing the line over for working the Pembroke & Tenby Railway Co., which was considered inexpedient". In view of the fact that the W&TV Chairman was none other than William Owen, it may be fair to say that he and J.J. Barrow did not see eye to eye. At any rate the W&TV remained independent and under local control, opening for freight on 24th March, 1873.

The vacancies on the P&T Board were taken by two men who were to give notable service to the company. One, W. Felix Poole, was associated with the railway for the rest of its history. The other, A.C. Sherriff, M.P. was involved for only a few years, but rapidly made his mark. Formerly the Traffic Manager of the North Eastern Railway, and successively General Manager of the Oxford, Worcester & Wolverhampton and West Midland Railways, his ability and experience was soon at work on behalf of the P&T. Before the end of 1871 he was seeking a £10,000 loan for the company, and by January 1872 he and J.J. Barrow were negotiating with the Midland Railway about exchange of traffic. Later in 1872 he joined Smedley in much of the work leading up to the agreement of 31st July, 1872, regarding traffic exchange with the Great Western. If Sherriff was the most experienced of the new men, there were others who were well qualified. Later in the 1870s H.S. Ellis, a Director of the Bristol & Exeter Railway, joined the Board of the P&T.

J.J. Barrow was now the largest shareholder in both the P&T and M&M companies. The idea of merging the two must have appealed to him, although ironically there is no sign of a serious attempt to do so until after 1st August, 1872, when P&T and M&M services became separated by over thirty miles of GWR and C&CR track. On 16th January, 1873, the Pembroke and Tenby Board met in London and received a report from A.C. Sherriff on "the policy of fusing the staffs of the two companies". The same report was received by the M&M Board at a meeting held on the same day at the same address, 6 Raymond Buildings. As the same four men — Barrow, Sherriff, Forster and Poole — constituted both Boards for both meetings it is not surprising that the companies did not argue! The report appears to have been accepted in part. At this stage no effort was made to fuse the locomotive, and carriage and wagon department, but general approval seems to have been given to the notion of having one Secretary and one Manager for both companies. In fact only the post of Secretary was merged in this way, and Mr Smedley of the P&T and Mr E. Hamer of the M&M continued in office as Managers of their respective railways. On 29th August, 1873 Thomas Stokes was given notice, and W. Felix Poole was appointed Secretary in his place. By March 1874, the P&T and the M&M had moved their offices to 15 The Parade, Carmarthen, and Poole was established there as Secretary to both companies. In order to accept the office Poole resigned his directorship in 1873; at about the same time G.E. Forster also resigned from the Board, becoming the company's solicitor in place of a local man, W. Davies.

Although Thomas Stokes was dismissed primarily to make way for Poole as Joint Secretary, his removal was a personal disaster. On 23rd December, 1873, the P&T Board recorded their desire "to state that Mr Stokes . . . as Secretary for fourteen years performed his duties with great courtesy to all concerned, and that arrangements with which he had nothing to do were the cause of his leaving the service." Only a month later Poole informed the Board of irregularities in the use of debenture bonds apparently attributable to Stokes. By the end of September 1874, the irregularities were described as "defalca-

A photograph said to be of the first locomotive arriving in Tenby, 1863.
R.E. Bowen Collection

An early picture of railwaymen and others in front of the locomotive *Milford*.
Tenby Museum

Locomotive 2–4–0 *Pembroke* at Newbury on a DN&S line train.

L.G.R.P., Courtesy David & Charles

The Wyman's bookstall on Tenby station, 1908.   *Tenby Museum*

The up side station buildings at Whitland.

British Rail

Narberth station, *c.*1920.

R.E. Bowen Collection

NARBERTH STATION

Templeton station, looking north. *R.E. Bowen*

Class 41xx 2–6–2T No. 4107 pauses at Saundersfoot station with a down train on 14th August, 1963. *M.R.C. Price*

Miners' train headed by Manning Wardle 0–4–0ST *Rosalind* (or *Roslyn*) in Railway Street, Saundersfoot **c.**1925.   *Mrs E. Skone*

Driver Bowen and colleagues on a GWR Mogul at Saundersfoot station, *c.*1936.   *R.E. Bowen*

Bonvilles Court Colliery in the Edwardian era. *Mrs D Evans*

0–4–0ST *Bulldog* of the Saundersfoot Railway leaves Bonvilles Court for Llanelly, July 1939. *M.R.C. Price Collection*

Passengers and railwaymen await a down train at Tenby. *Mrs E. Skone*

The south sands, Tenby, at the turn of the century. *M.R.C. Price Collection*

Valentine's Series

South Sands, Tenby 1408

Dean Goods 0–6–0 No. 2407 at Tenby in June 1932.   *R. Daniells*

Station staff at Tenby.   *Tenby Museum*

Tenby station, looking north. Note the second track over the viaduct in use as a carriage siding. *O.P.C. Collection*

"Hall" class 4–6–0 No. 5976 *Ashwicke Hall* leaves Tenby with a train for Pembroke Dock, 14th August, 1963. *M.R.C. Price*

Tenby Lower Yard, the site of the first Tenby station and the P&TR's works and locomotive shed, 14th August, 1963. *M.R.C. Price*

Black Rock Quarry, Tenby in the late nineteenth century. *British Rail*

A down train passes Black Rock, south of Tenby.   *M.R.C. Price Collection*

The station buildings at Penally.   *R.E. Bowen*

Camping coach behind the down platform, Manorbier. Camping coaches were also situated at Saundersfoot, Tenby and Penally. *British Rail*

Manorbier station, looking west. *O.P.C. Collection*

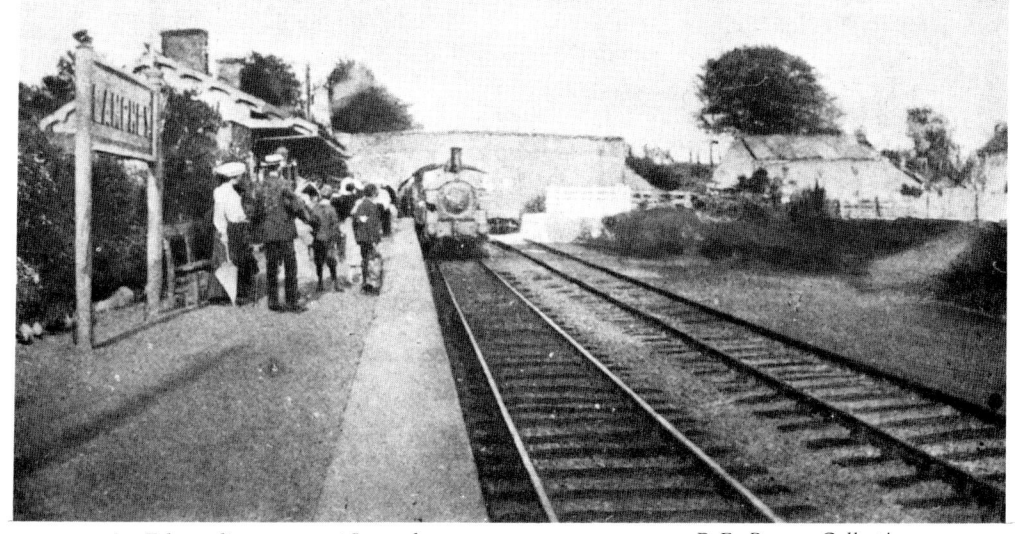

Lamphey Station, Pembrokeshire.
Morgan, Pembroke Dock.

An Edwardian scene at Lamphey. *R.E. Bowen Collection*

Steam railcar No. 48 with tail load at Lamphey. *H.C. Casserley Collection*

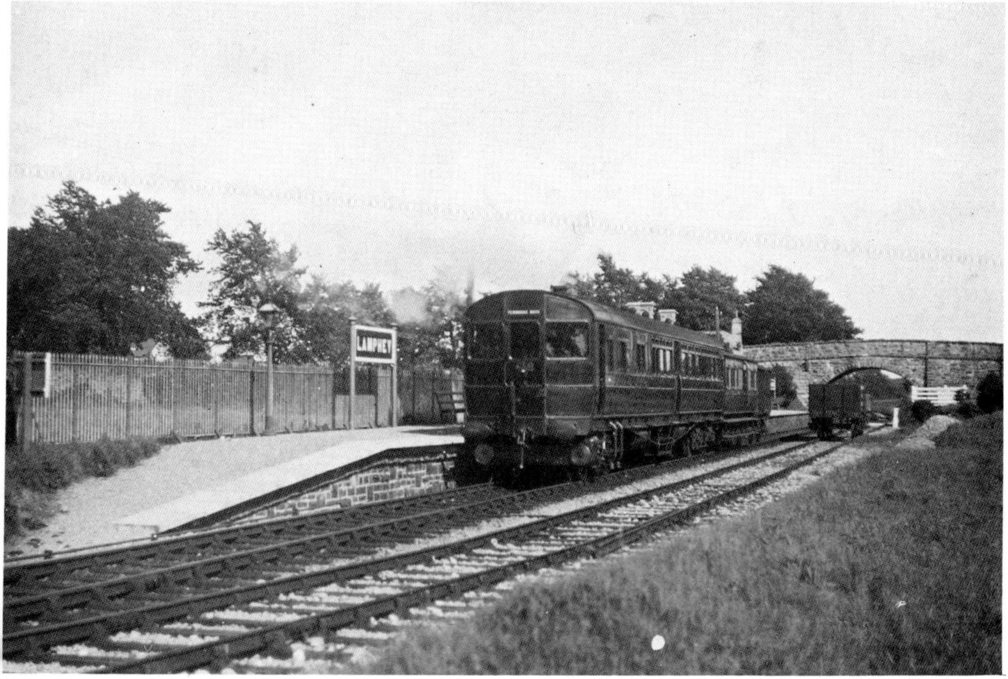
LAMPHEY

Steam railcar No. 68 labelled *Tenby & Whitland* climbs from Pembroke Dock towards Pembroke tunnel.
E.R. Mountford Collection

0–6–0ST locomotive and Dean 0–6–0 on a troop train approaching Pembroke tunnel in the early years of this century.
Real Photographs

Llanion crossing, Pembroke Dock.   *R.E. Bowen Collection*

Hobbs Point, with the Naval dockyard beyond.   *M.R.C. Price Collection*

Exterior of Pembroke Dock station. *H.C. Casserley Collection*

DMU at the renovated Pembroke Dock station, September, 1980.
M.R.C. Price

tions", totalling £2140, on the issue of five debenture stock bonds. There was no suggestion of prosecution, however. The Board simply agreed to accept a repayment of £982 10s. 0d. in cash, and the balance by instalments of £25 per annum.

In view of Stokes' activities, combining the post of Secretary of the two companies was an especially good move for the P&T. In an informal sense, the post of Engineer was already combined, of course, although J.W. Szlumper seems to have found his P&T office rather onerous. Replying to company correspondence on 24th February, 1874, he said that he considered his duties as Engineer to the two companies to be superintending the maintenance and renewal of permanent way, and examining the line bridges, culverts and other structures. He accepted responsibility for signals, stations and yards, and for superintending men engaged on the works. Amongst other things he also had to make the necessary returns to the Board of Trade, and give the usual half-yearly Engineers' certificate. Although he claimed these duties were becoming more demanding, he deferred a request for a salary increase "until the lines are in a more prosperous state". At the same time Szlumper wrote "it would be advantageous if my duties on the P&TR could be carried out without the interference of any other official whose duties are in an entirely different department" — a blow aimed surely at Isaac Smedley, whose original title "Traffic Manager" belied the extent of his activities.

Szlumper may have had reason to complain. To judge from his first report in 1869 he may have supposed that he had charge of the rolling stock. In fact the responsibility belonged to Smedley, who was assisted by Richard Metcalf of the locomotive department. Again, from time to time Szlumper found he was sharing work on buildings with Smedley. In November, 1872, for instance, both men were asked to obtain tenders for a carriage shed at Pembroke Dock, and at the same period they were equally involved in plans for a pontoon at Hobbs Point. Probably Szlumper disliked Smedley's power if not his person, and it is possible to speculate that tension between the two men may have been a factor inhibiting the Directors from giving the capable Smedley management powers on the M&M in 1873. Evidence is lacking, and at this date no doubt other factors prevented the fusion of M&M and P&T staff. Even so the new men plainly hoped for it. Under J.J. Barrow's leadership they were on their way to building a modest railway empire. Although the Whitland & Taf Vale had gone its own way, the P&T and the M&M had become brothers if not twins. Even more remarkable, they had a cousin in the English Home Counties. This was the Hemel Hempstead Railway, a company formed to build a line between Harpenden on the Midland Railway and Hemel Hempstead. John Barrow had become involved in it in 1862, and he and his son provided a very large part of the capital. By 1872 the Board of the Hemel Hempstead Railway included some familiar names — Sherriff, Poole, Ellis and also C.L. Denton, who replaced G.E. Forster on the P&T Board in 1873. As a team of railway Directors, these men can only be called the Barrow boys!

Estimate of Expense letter of 1858.

Chapter Seven
The P & T at Pembroke Dock

Naval shipbuilding at Pembroke Dock reached a peak in the 1850s and, although there was some decline in the 1860s, up to 3,000 men were employed at the Royal Dockyard in the years prior to 1865. Amongst the vessels built in this period were the *Conflict* (1846), the first ship to be fitted with a screw propeller, and the *Duke of Wellington* (1852), reputedly the largest three deck man-of-war ever built. As a result Pembroke Dock was an industrial town before the P & T was born, and important enought to have a sizeable Army garrison. Even so the Admiralty regarded the early railway schemes with mixed feelings. Although the vastly improved communications offered by the railways were attractive, almost every railway promoter also wanted to develop commercial docks on Milford Haven. This must have looked like the thin end of a large wedge: doubtless the dreams of a new Liverpool in west Wales seemed as plausible to the admirals as they did to everyone else. The prospect of commercial shipping cluttering up the Haven did not please them.

The P & T's 1859 Act envisaged that the western terminus of the railway would be at Hobbs Point on Milford Haven. As has been seen, the government was slow to make land available, and the original powers for this short section appear to have expired. In any event provision for the Hobbs Point branch was made in the P & T's 1866 Act, which estimated that the cost of a double line 54½ chains long would be no less than £44,000! Of this total, earthworks accounted for £8,542 and the wharf for £8750; land was estimated at £3442, permanent way at £2997, and a station at £1000. The sum of £6959 for contingencies suggests that James Mathias, the Engineer, could hardly be certain of the final cost! In the event finding the finance was not an immediate problem because the Admiralty raised objections to the works. Only after an extension of time for the works had been sought in 1869, and after the dockyard extension line had been approved in 1870, was there some movement in the situation.

David Davies' liability to build the Hobbs Point line under his 1862 contract gave rise to some debate, but eventually Davies offered to tackle the job for £16,000 in fully paid up preference shares. On 3rd February, 1871, the contractor was asked to start the work, and he did so, even though the Admiralty had not agreed to allow the pier to be extended to deep water. One of the first tasks was the construction of a sea wall to secure the side of the line where it ran adjacent to west Llanion Pill. The foundation stone for this wall was laid on 12th July, 1871, and as the wall took shape it had the additional benefit of protecting the flood-prone Water Street from water!

As built the junction for the single track branch was 17 chains east of Pembroke Dock station, and the line itself was 51 chains long. The falling gradients varied from 1 in 85 near the junction to 1 in 58 nearer the wharf, and on the way there were two level crossings, the main one at Water Street. The line ended at Hobbs Point in several sidings: wagon turntables were installed and freight facilities only were provided.

Although the works were not entirely finished, the Hobbs Point branch was ready for use by the beginning of April, 1872. Mentioning the opening the *Welshman* reported "The trucks run direct to the new pier, where they can be discharged or loaded from vessels alongside. Ample lifting power has been provided, including a steam crane. There is also a tip for the shipping of coal and culm." The details in this description may have been somewhat premature, because an order for a steam crane capable of lifting 5 tons was not placed until May, and the design of a large coal tip at Hobbs Point was still under discussion in July. By September 1872, however, a weighbridge for loads up to 20 tons had been erected, and the Directors resolved that a wooden shed should be put up to protect the steam crane.

As built the wharf could accommodate only small vessels with a shallow draught. The Admiralty repeatedly objected to the extention of the pier into deep water, and so the P&T proposed the use of pontoons instead. This idea was not greeted with any more enthusiasm. On 15th July, 1872, the Pembroke Dock committee noted that F.L. Clark and W.F. Poole had shown plans of the pontoons to the Commandant of H.M. Dockyard. The Admiralty refused to be impressed. Further negotiations took place in 1873, but by the end of the year it was decided that they should stand over "until it is seen whether Mr Reed's company at Jacobs Pill require a railway to be made". E.J. Reed was Chief Constructor of the Navy 1863–1870, and prospective Liberal candidate for Pembroke Boroughs, a seat he actually won at the General Election of February 1874. In 1873, however, he had decided to set up his own shipyard at Jacobs Pill, on the Pembroke River. It does not appear to have been a great success. Some iron caissons used in the construction of Milford Docks were built at Jacob's Pill, and in 1877 the yard launched a corvette for the Japanese government. The Japanese ambassador and his entourage travelled by train to Pembroke Dock for the ceremony, but this rather exotic occasion seems to have marked the zenith of the shipyard's fortunes. The P&T was never pressed to build a railway to the yard, which appears to have closed in about 1881. Significantly, perhaps, Mr Reed was by then representing Cardiff in Parliament.

Throughout the 1870s the P&T Directors were concerned about extending Hobbs Point pier to deep water. In August, 1874, they brought in a civil engineer called Abernethy to report on the possibilities. Two months later he was asked to confer with the Admiralty, but it was not until 16th November, 1875, that the Board heard that the Admiralty had approved plans for an extension 500 feet from the government pier. Even then progress was slow, and the P&T's papers do not refer to a tender for the job until 1st June, 1877! In the meantime Abernethy's plan had been amended somewhat, enabling a row to develop over the civil engineer's fees. On 30th August, 1878, Messrs Jones & Johns of Pembroke Dock put in a tender of £20,566 for the works. This figure must have been too high because in October of that year the P&T consulted another firm of contractors, Messrs Appleby & Lawton. Negotiations dragged on, and in April 1880 Appleby & Lawton were asked to make a new estimate. By then the P&T was more impoverished, and there is no sign that the scheme was ever completed. It is believed that Appleby & Lawton executed a few improvements at this period, but they were too little and too late. Commercially Hobbs Point pier was never a great success.

The history of the Dockyard Extension, the P&T's other line at Pembroke Dock, is not without its vicissitudes. Initially the P&T was reluctant to build the extension because the Admiralty was so unco-operative over arrangements at Hobbs Point. Indeed, on 18th October, 1866, the Board resolved to postpone any continuation of the line into the Royal dockyard until the Admiralty was willing for works authorised in the 1866 Act to proceed. The stalemate was not broken until 1869, when the resumption of negotiations may have owed something to the arrival on the scene of the Barrows. In any event, the P&T's Act of 1870 provided for the building of the Dockyard Extension, and the required capital appears to have been raised by the issue of Dockyard Guaranteed Stock on which the Admiralty agreed to pay an annuity. The 1870 Act also embodied an agreement made on 31st March, 1870, between the P&T and the Admiralty dealing with the use of the Extension. Under it the P&T was permitted to use the new line for all purposes connected with the traffic of the dockyard, and was free to operate over that part of the Extension outside the dockyard for the general traffic of the company. Evidently the P&T was responsible for maintaining 200 yards of track inside the dockyard, and it was agreed that the company should receive 3d./ton net on all goods and merchandise conveyed over the line.

Construction of the Extension necessitated the demolition of a number of dwellings, and so it cannot be said that the scheme was very popular locally. However, land for the Extension was purchased by November 1870, and work went ahead under the supervision of the Engineer, J.W. Szlumper. Following a rather sinuous course through the town, the line descended on gradients as severe as 1 in 44 for about 20 chains before climbing just as steeply to the dockyard gates, 37 chains from Pembroke Dock station. In this short distance there were no less than six level crossings: needless to say it was a line to be worked with care! The Dockyard Extension was opened for regular traffic on 21st July, 1871, although it may have seen some use for perhaps two months previously. Before long an argument arose between the P&T and the Admiralty over the cost of maintaining the railway, and persisted for four years in spite of the March 1870 agreement. Eventually on 7th January, 1876, the arbitrator, Mr Brady of the South Eastern Railway decided that the Admiralty should pay £321 for maintenance between 21st July, 1871 and 30th April, 1875, and proposed payments rising to £94 p.a. to cover the ensuing years.

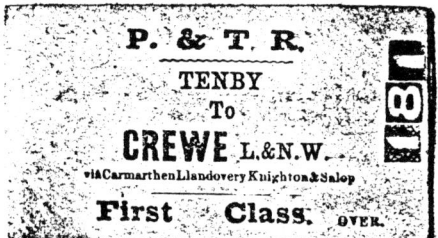

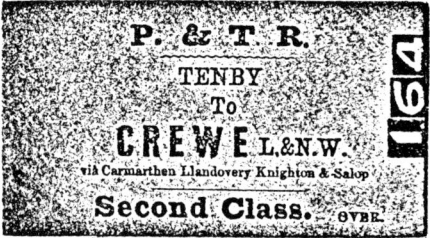

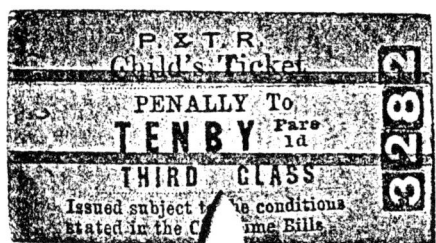

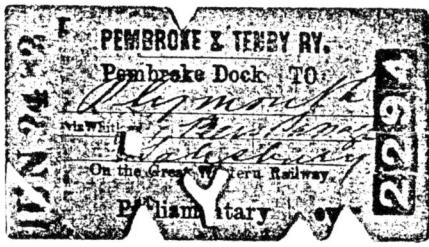

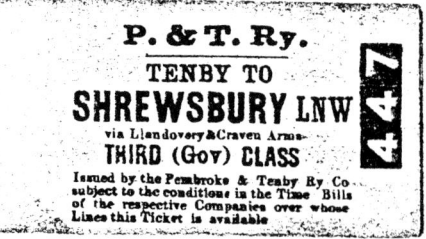

Chapter Eight
Consolidation and Crisis

In many ways the years between 1874 and 1882 were a pivotal period for the Pembroke & Tenby Railway. Prior to 1874 the story was one of expansion, optimism and even modest prosperity; after 1874 the growth was checked, and a few years of consolidation gave way to increasing financial anxiety. Such a change in the company's fortunes reflected economic conditions in the country more than innovations by the new directorate. However, it might be said that, whilst David Davies was fortunate and shrewd in his administration, the Barrows were less fortunate and perhaps over-optimistic in theirs. In 1874, though, they could still look to the future and hope for the fulfilment of the Manchester & Milford Haven dream. Unfortunately for them it was not then obvious that dreaming would be to no avail.

Before enlarging on this theme, a variety of other matters deserve to be noticed, and the first of these is the P&T's relations with local industry. By supporting the P&T Acts of 1864 and 1866 the industrialist C.R. Vickerman had hoped to see the company take an interest in serving his collieries. In the event the P&T did little, even though it had obtained powers to link up with the Saundersfoot Railway. Only the Moreton colliery was provided with a siding, but this pit did not belong to C.R. Vickerman; significantly no doubt, Moreton happened to be a principal supplier of coal to the Pembroke & Tenby Railway. In addition the first Saundersfoot station was constructed at Moreton rather than Bonvilles Court, C.R. Vickerman's main colliery. This was adding insult to injury, because the Moreton site was thoroughly inconvenient for Vickerman, and for many less prominent residents.

Complaints about the station site soon met with success. In 1868 the station (which apparently consisted of little more than a wooden hut) was moved to the present site, not far from Bonvilles Court. Before long there were fresh complaints — this time about the inadequacy of the station's facilities. Vickerman backed these, and renewed his own grumble about the P&T failing to provide a standard gauge link with Bonvilles Court. Years later he summed it all up by saying the P&T "favoured a small hitherto unprofitable colliery (Moreton) and left three large expensive collieries out in the cold". The P&T was not impressed. It provided an exchange siding with the Saundersfoot Railway at the new Saundersfoot station, and decided that was the most the traffic deserved, and the most the P&T could afford. The company's attitude is not hard to understand. The Pembrokeshire coalfield was notoriously unreliable, suffering especially from faulting and flooding, and by Glamorgan standards all the mines were small. The outlay of £8,000 (as estimated in 1873) for a branch to Bonvilles Court was more than the company could risk.

Instead the P&T suggested the colliery company should build the branch itself. C.R. Vickerman thought otherwise, and in 1873 and 1874 he modernised the Saundersfoot Railway. Much of the track was relaid, and the Manning Wardle 0–4–0ST *Rosalind* (or *Roslyn*) was acquired to work between Bonvilles Court incline and the harbour. Horses continued to haul trains on the section between Bonvilles Court and the Saundersfoot station exchange siding.

At the same period an interesting but obscure experiment in motive power was being conducted at Moreton Colliery. According to the local press a "trucking machine" was introduced in April, 1874, to take coal from the colliery to Saundersfoot station. The machine was described as "powerful, but light and elegant". Unfortunately exact details of the design cannot be determined: at different dates the patentee, David Parsell, devised a compressed air locomotive and also a vertical boiler steam engine equipped with a kind of condensing apparatus. The trucking machine may well have been of the latter type, because on one occasion it is said to have run through to Tenby — an excursion which was probably impractical for a locomotive of the other design evidently dependent on a pipe line adjacent to the track to enable compressed air pressure to be maintained. In any event it is likely that the trucking machine was of local construction: Parsell had an interest in the Woodside Foundry near Saundersfoot, and this turned out such a range of castings and equipment for local industry that this job was probably within its capabilities.

In the meantime, P&T operations were somewhat marred by a number of mishaps. The first accident on the line after the company became respnsible for working occurred on 9th August, 1872. The engine in charge of the 10 o'clock up passenger train left the rails on the approach to Saundersfoot station, but fortunately no one was hurt. A few weeks later, however, on 20th September, the guard of a goods train was killed at Manorbier. This attracted the concern of the Board of Trade, but a verdict of accidental death was returned at the inquest. A similar verdict was recorded after an accident in September 1874, when a man was killed on the railway at Lamphey.

Although there was no fatality, an accident with more serious implications for the company occurred at Whitland on 17th January, 1876. A break in a shunting rope at Narberth caused two loaded coal wagons to run away down the gradient to Whitland. Porters Thomas and Lewis were carried off with the wagons and, having made frantic but unsuccessful efforts to apply the brakes, they jumped clear on the approach to Whitland. A warning message had been delayed by a breakdown in the telegraph, and the runaway wagons crashed into a P&T passenger train standing in the station. Three people (including Lewis) were hurt, and the two wagons and the engine of the passenger train were said to be "somewhat damaged".

At the next Board meeting on 28th January the Engineer was asked to prepare an estimate for alterations at Narberth to prevent any similar mishap. In the event it seems that the views of the Board of Trade carried most weight, and alterations were made at Whitland also, ensuring that any runaway could be diverted well away from the GWR main line. Meanwhile even before the accident there had been plans afoot to install the single needle telegraph on the P&T line. In 1875 these were deferred on financial grounds, but on 17th August, 1876, Smedley was able to tell the Board that the single needle telegraph was being installed, to be used in conjunction with the staff and ticket system. In November 1876 a block instrument for use in relation to the P&TR was installed in the GWR box at Whitland. Such alterations must have pleased the Great Western, which had been pressing the P&T ever since the end of the broad gauge to co-operate in improving facilities at Whitland. Arguments over costs had caused delays, and some works were outstanding at the time of the 1876 crash.

Throughout the 1870s buildings and other railway facilities were gradually improved. On 15th July, 1872, the Pembroke Dock committee approved the construction of a platform between Penally and Manorbier "for the convenience of the visitors to the Lydstep caverns". This was probably in use within a matter of months, and was certainly open in 1874. That summer it was advertised that, on notice to the guard, trains would stop at Lydstep to set down Pic Nic or Pleasure parties of not less than six persons. In September, 1874, the company decided to build a small wooden shed for locomotive repairs at the P&T's original Tenby terminus, which became known as Tenby Lower Yard. It is thought that at this date there was already one small shed for locomotives at Tenby, in addition to small sheds at Pembroke Dock and Whitland, so the new shed indicated an enlargement of the amenities. In any event, it was completed in February 1875, and provided with redundant track from the main line, part of which was then being relaid. Soon after the Lower Yard saw the construction of new workshops for locomotive fitting, carriage and wagon repairs and painting; these were completed by February 1878. Apart from these developments, other improvements were modest. Numerous complaints about Saundersfoot station, and other criticisms about Narberth station did not meet with a rapid response. In 1878 plans were prepared for new stations at Saundersfoot and Kilgetty, but no action was taken. In July 1877, however, it was decided to build a new station at Narberth. The building cost £550, and was opened to passengers on 1st July, 1878. Evidently business at Narberth was expanding because in 1877 two extra cattle pens were

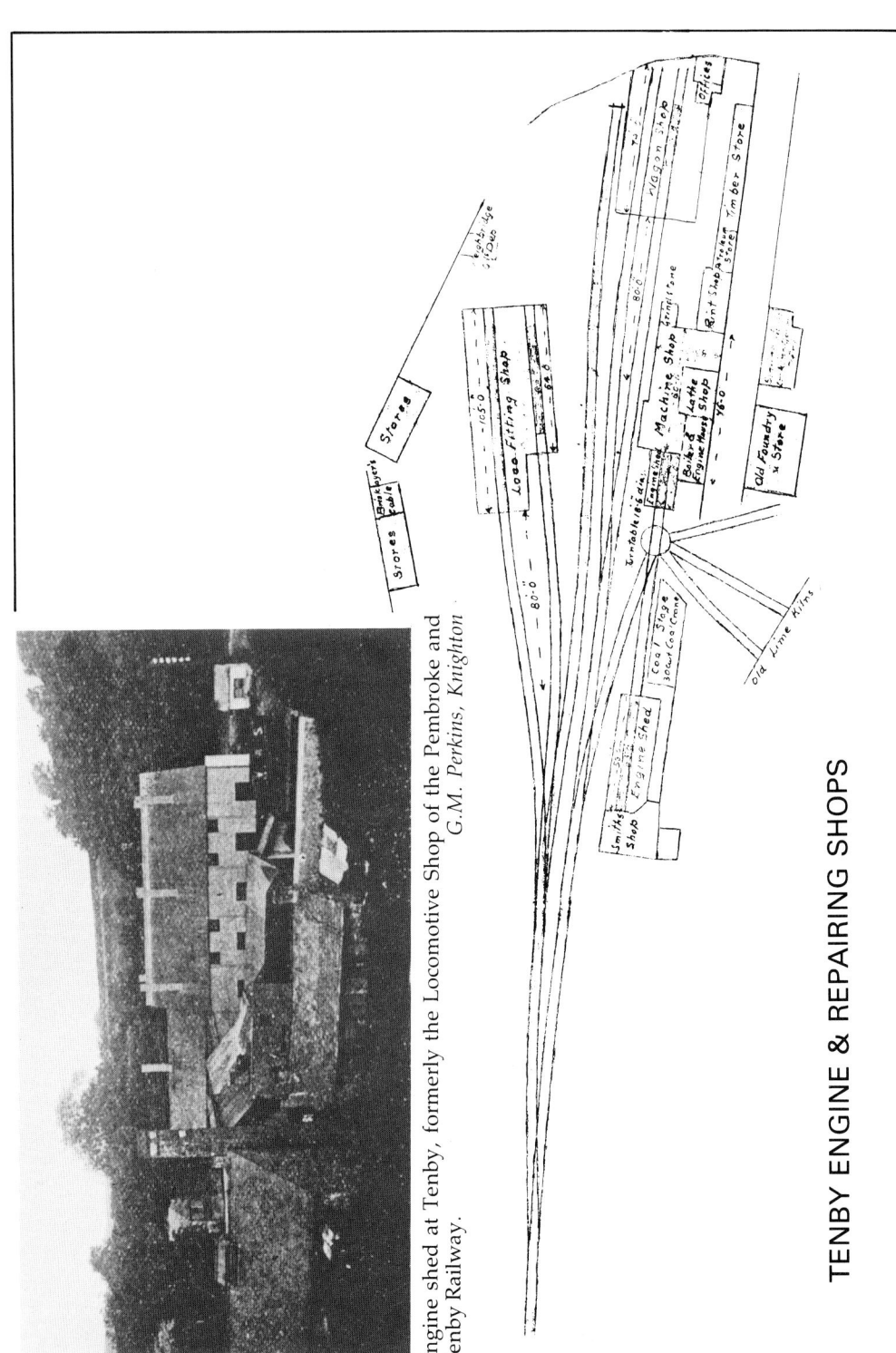

Engine shed at Tenby, formerly the Locomotive Shop of the Pembroke and
Tenby Railway.

G.M. Perkins, Knighton

TENBY ENGINE & REPAIRING SHOPS

ordered, and in June, 1878 a goods shed costing £40 was authorised.

Possibly Narberth was the only place to witness growth at this period: to judge from the figures for traffic exchanged with the GWR the growth of P&T traffic slowed considerably after 1874, except in the year to 31st July, 1877. By 1876 the company seems to have been feeling the pinch, because Board minutes of the period regularly record bank overdrafts ranging between £3000 and £7000: little wonder that capital investment was limited! On the brighter side, though, the P&T's timetable showed some improvements. The timetable for October 1877, advertised six trains down from Whitland and five up from Pembroke Dock, one of which terminated at Tenby. On Sundays there was one train between Pembroke Dock and Tenby at 3 pm returning from Tenby at 8 pm. All trains were booked to stop at all stations, but the No. 4 up train and No. 5 down train appear to have been regarded as fast because they stopped at Kilgetty & Begelly only on prior notice to the guard. Templeton station earned a mention only in the timetable notes, from which the traveller learned that "The No. 1 down train will call on Fridays when Market Tickets will be issued to Pembroke Dock at 2s. 7d. each: also the No. 1 and No. 2 down on Saturdays to Tenby 1s. 3d.: Pembroke 2s. 3d. Returning both days by No. 3 and No. 4 up trains." From this it would seem that the P&T officially prevented a passenger travelling from Templeton to Whitland, or any station off the P&T!

Whatever its attitude to Templeton passengers, the P&T was well aware of the need to advertise connecting services. At least three-quarters of the October, 1877 timetable poster was devoted to such timings, mostly at stations on the GWR, LNWR or Midland Railways. Connecting times to and from stations on the C&C and M&M were given, but Haverfordwest (GWR) was accorded the greatest honour with details of connection via Whitland and via Pembroke Dock. Although use of the Hobbs Point–New Milford ferry was an essential ingredient in the latter journey the post made a point of telling travellers that "A steamer will leave Hobbs Point for Neyland at 8.30 pm daily until further notice — wind and weather permitting." In slightly smaller type the word "Omnibuses" was printed, and these were said to meet trains at Narberth, Saundersfoot, Tenby, Pembroke and Pembroke Dock. The remarkable amount of timetable space devoted to connections suggests not only that the P&T encouraged through traffic but also that the company realised south Pembrokeshire had plenty of attractions for visitors. The opening of Lydstep platform was certainly an early sign of good appreciation of tourism. Even so the company had its financial worries, and they did not diminish as the decade went on. The Directors, indeed became more and more concerned to make economies.

Against this background there were new proposals for a merger between the P&T and M&M. As the latter company was facing similar and more actute difficulties this was a natural step for two companies with close associations. However the signs are that J.J. Barrow was becoming more and more disenchanted with his railways. Far from dominating a great flow of traffic between Manchester and Milford Haven, he found himself at the head of two isolated undertakings wallowing in a mire of deteriorating finances. In these circumstances he appears to have become utterly fed up, and in February 1879, he resigned from the chair of both companies. According to the minutes of the P&T Board his resignation was "reluctantly accepted". His replacement as Chairman of both railways was actually his next door neighbour in Westbourne Terrace, London, W. Eagle Bott. He had joined the Board of the P&T in August, 1878 and the Board of the M&M two months later. Very likely Bott was a personal friend of J.J. Barrow, and seen as an able man ready to devote his energies to these struggling railways. At any rate his first move was to take a fresh look at the idea of unifying their management.

On 13th June, 1879, the P&T Board met at 22 Conduit Place, Paddington, and received a report entitled "General Position of the company". At the same time a similar report was presented to the M&M Board, and the outcome was the setting up of an M&M and P&T joint committee. This was given the task of "ascertaining additional economy of management to reduce annual expenses consistent with efficiency". The committee first met on 24th June, and comprised W. Eagle Bott, J.J. Barrow and another Director, C.S. Williams. They agreed to give six months notice to the principal heads of department — Isaac Smedley, Manager of the P&T, E. Hamer, his counterpart on the M&M, and J.W. Szlumper, Engineer to both railways. This step was not quite as drastic as it might seem: there had been internal difficulties on the M&M in relation to the Manager and the Engineer, and the intention now was to appoint Smedley as General Manager of both lines. In the interim the committee members decided to visit the railways personally "to study on the spot the utility of suggested alterations, and especially to inspect the permanent way and engineering shops". The visit evidently confirmed their suspicions: the permanent way was not in the condition expected, and they felt that both companies would benefit "on all subjects" by unity of management and combination of departments. The development of combined workshops at Carmarthen was tentatively contemplated, and with the Secretary, W.F. Poole, already at Carmarthen it was agreed that the offices of both companies should be centralised there.

A longer report from the joint committee was put before the P&T Board on 12th December, 1879. It argued again "that the management ought to be under one head, carried out with one staff, that the Secretary ought also to act as Treasurer, drawing all cheques, and making all payments, so far relieving the traffic management from all such details". It also revealed some of the existing problems: "the present mode of ordering materials (i.e. stores) is most inconvenient, unbusiness-like and unusual. It appears that the Traffic Managers and the Engineer have been in the habit of ordering articles except rails, sleepers and coal at will; also large repairs to rolling stock without any consultation with the Directors on the subject." This was obviously a sore point, and made no better by the realisation that clerks had also been appointed and discharged without consultation. With manifest irritation the committee declared "in short . . . the Directors have had a minimum voice in the management of the lines, instead of being consulted on all subjects". The main recommendation was that three Directors should constitute a Locomotive Stores and General Management Committee whose proceedings should be reported to subsequent Board meetings.

The P&T Board approved this report unanimously, giving the joint committee full powers to carry out its recommendations. One of these had been for the railways to put in charge of the locomotive and carriage and wagon departments "a practical man of mechanical knowledge and permanent way experience" — surely a comment on the expertise of Szlumper, if not of Smedley! On 12th December, 1879 with Szlumper's term due to end on 31st December, Lionel B. Wood of the North Eastern Railway, was appointed superintendent of the locomotive department, of carriage and wagon repairs, and engineer of the permanent way. His salary of £300 p.a. was to be paid by the P&T and M&M in equal shares, and he was told to devote "his whole time and energy to the interests of the two companies".

By March 1880, the reforms were being put into effect. Orders had been placed for three months supplies of materials, and plans were afoot for the joint purchase of stores six months ahead. Bott paid a further visit to both railways to "further the changes already introduced". Hardly had the process begun, however, before a crisis arose in the affairs of the M&MR. Both Hamer and Szlumper felt aggrieved by their dismissal, and Szlumper perhaps especially so, because in 1879 he had also lost his job as Engineer to the Whitland & Cardigan Railway. In 1880 Szlumper turned to litigation, and as regards the P&T was not satisfied until the company made a payment into court in 1881. To make matters worse, in 1880 one of the M&MR's creditors, the Cambrian Railways, petitioned in Chancery for the Milford company to be put into liquidation. In August 1880, the court appointed a barrister, Mr J.C. Russell, to be Manager of the M & M, and in November 1880 he was also made Receiver, to take over financial administration from Felix Poole. In fact he did no work as Receiver until February 1881.

The intervention of the court entirely disrupted the joint committee's plans, and deepened the sense of crisis. In October 1880, Russell gave notice to the new Engineer L.B. Wood and reappointed Szlumper as Engineer of the M & MR. The Board protested, and there were allegations of misconduct against the Directors. Russell's popularity with the Directors was not improved by his dealings with Smedley, whose appointment as General Manager of both lines had been confirmed by the joint committee in February, 1880. In spite of Russell's appointment, Smedley continued to act as Manager of the M & MR, but in January 1881 he was given notice to take effect on 31st March. Ironically, before he left he managed to reach an agreement with the Cambrian Railways regarding the M & M's outstanding debts on its disused line between Llanidloes and Llangurig in Mid-Wales.

When the joint committee met on 3rd December, 1880, there was scarcely a reference to all the changes boldly envisaged a year earlier. More trivial matters were mentioned instead, like the possible sale of surplus land at Tenby. However, the Directors were told that a private Bill was being promoted to permit the sale of the Carmarthen & Cardigan Railway to the GWR. This must have been the last straw, because any plan for amalgamation, or even co-operation, between the M & M and P & T would be very much at the mercy of the Great Western. The Bill was passed, though, and on 1st July, 1881, the C & CR became part of the GWR. By now there was little left for the joint committee to do, and the final meeting, held on 21st March, 1882, dealt with minor financial matters only.

Chapter Nine
The Last Years

The troubles of the Manchester & Milford evidently depressed W. Eagle Bott as much as they had depressed J.J. Barrow. At the end of 1880 Bott resigned as Chairman because "the duties and responsibilities of the office were undefined by the court whilst Mr. Russell assumed and claimed it". The events of 1881 did nothing to boost Bott's morale, and in May 1882 he resigned as Chairman of the P&TR. On 12th July, 1882 the Board unanimously voted J.J. Barrow back into the P&T chair: his re-appointment marked the start of the final phase of the company's independent career. Even so, it took a while for the dust to settle after Bott's departure because there was an argument over his large claim for expenses. This was not too protracted, but the next half-yearly shareholders meeting approved a resolution that no Director should receive more expenses than the sum annually voted for the purpose. At the time this was £300 free of tax, but inclusive of all travelling expenses. Set alongside the earnings of some of the staff such expenses seem generous indeed, and it becomes hard to see the P&T Board as benevolent, bearing in mind that in October 1882 the Directors deferred an application by numerous employees for wage increases of 1/- per week! The P&T men may not have been so badly off, though: in the same month some of the Whitland & Cardigan Railway's staff appealed to their management for parity with P&T employees!

Unlike the M&M, the P&T emerged from the crisis of 1879–1881 still capable of standing on its own feet. The P&T Board was no longer divided into Pembroke Dock and London committees, but unified behind J.J. Barrow and his son J.B. Barrow. The other Directors in January 1883 were F.L. Clark, C.S. Williams and W. Wavell. Although the company was by no means wealthy, some capital expenditure could be considered with Barrow family backing. In July 1882 the Engineer was asked to investigate the possible purchase of a six coupled tank engine and, although in September he referred to taking an engine on trial, four months later the matter was in the hands of the Chairman and David Davies, who, incidentally, had objected to the 1879 merger scheme. Eventually, in October 1883 agreement was reached for the purchase of an engine from the GWR. J.J. Barrow found £1,200 and Davies contributed £800; the engine was named *Holmwood*. Doubtless encouraged by this transaction, in 1884 the P&T negotiated with the GWR for the purchase of another locomotive. On 27th February, 1885 it was reported that the engine *Stella*, had been received and was working satisfactorily. This time the cost was charged to Revenue account, although on the same day the Chairman proposed the issue of £20,000 Preference shares unissued under the 1866 Act for the purpose of completing certain works at Hobbs Point and increasing rolling stock.

Repeated complaints reminded the Board that improvements were required at Saundersfoot and Kilgetty. As usual C.R. Vickerman lead the protesters, describing the wooden shed removed to Saundersfoot from Moreton Colliery as "a disgrace to your railway". In May, 1882 the Directors sanctioned the erection of a shelter on Saundersfoot's up platform at a cost not exceeding £70. On 24th June Mr Vickerman wrote to express the residents' disappointment at the lack of progress in providing "an improved and suitable station . . . beyond some trifling excavation for a wooden open shed on the up line". A further complaint in February 1885 produced no better result. In February 1887, however, the P&T Chairman was petitioned by Saundersfoot people, and on 20th July the Directors finally agreed to the construction of new corrugated iron stations, both at Saundersfoot and at Kilgetty. Outlay on the two was limited to £250, and the contract for construction was given to I. Dixon & Co. of Liverpool. The work was soon in hand and, on 15th December, 1887, the Board was told that the station buildings were completed and open for traffic.

Improvements were being made at other places on the railway. At Tenby a new station approach road was laid in the mid 1880s, and in 1887 the Tenby Gas Consumer Company presented the Directors with a lamp standard for the approach road, inscribed to commemorate Queen Victoria's Golden Jubilee. This survived until the station was rebuilt in 1959. At Pembroke meanwhile, £150 was allowed in 1882 to enable a new siding to be laid. In 1890 a new iron goods shed was constructed at Pembroke, and in the following year it was decided to build two houses at Pembroke Station at an estimated cost of £120 each. Compared with the cost of the siding, this figure seems to offer some comment on the quality of housing!

At Whitland alterations to the engine shed were proposed. In November 1881 the Engineer suggested the provision of water tanks and other equipment in Whitland goods yard to give the P&T a water supply independent of the GWR. Isaac Smedley was authorised to negotiate, and emerged with satisfactory terms for the P&T; from 1st January, 1881, the company had to pay £40 per annum for the use of the Great Western's water supply. Five years later the boot was on the other foot. The GWR began working the Whitland & Cardigan line from 1st September, 1886, but wanted to use a shed at Whitland in preference to the W&CR shed at Llanfalteg. They negotiated with the P&T and, for the significant rent of £40 per annum, were allowed to use the P&T's shed and turntable for an initial period of two years.

In 1886 the Board of Trade expressed concern about the P&T's practice of running mixed trains, and asked that if the practice was really necessary, carriages be put behind goods trucks and not next to the engine. Smedley did not think it practicable for the P & T to oblige considering the company's circumstances and the character of its traffic. Unfortunately the Board of Trade response is not recorded! The Manager must have been better pleased with new terms negotiated for the carriage of mails: in August, 1887 the rate was increased by £50 p.a. to £150 p.a. In the same month the passenger timetable showed no less than seven trains each way on weekdays. Of these two could reasonably be called "fast", the 5.45 pm down calling only at Tenby, Pembroke and Pembroke Dock, whilst the 9.30 am up called at Pembroke, Tenby and Saundersfoot. Both these trains conveyed Paddington through coaches worked via the recently opened Severn Tunnel. One train, the 2.30 pm from Pembroke Dock, terminated at Tenby. On Sundays there was a train in each direction, leaving Pembroke Dock at 3.00 pm and returning from Whitland at 7.00 pm. In the summer of 1887 the improved service of through coaches proved so popular that the arrangement was repeated in subsequent summers from 1st July to 30th September inclusive. Tourism was increasing in Pembrokeshire, and Tenby in particular was popular.

Whilst on the subject of train services, brief mention of the P & T's tickets may be of interest. First class single tickets were coloured white, second class singles were mauve and third class singles were either buff or green; Parliamentary and Government tickets were also green. A child's third class single ticket was more colourful, having yellow horizontal bands with two horizontal lines. Nowadays few P & T return tickets survive, but it appears that first class returns were yellow on the return (left hand) half, and red on the outward (right hand) half. Second class tickets were coloured mauve on the left half and blue or red on the right half. Third class tickets were green on the left half and white or yellow on the right. An Officer's ticket, first class, was white on both halves, and a tourist first class return was pink on the left and white on the right. Market tickets were green on the left and white or brown on the right, whilst an express train return was pink on the left and red on the right. Special excursion tickets were often embellished with colourful vertical stripes. So far as is known, all P & T tickets were standard Edmondson cards. Early issues were blank on the reverse, but later some had conditions printed on the back. Tickets to stations off the company's line carried through journey conditions, whilst tickets to Ireland had very lengthy conditions with the additional note: "Not available by limited Mail train unless stated in the Coy's Timetable and Notices to be so". Other tickets referred to the conditions of issue only on the face of the ticket.

One part of the P&TR requiring no public passenger tickets was the Dockyard Extension railway. Its fortunes fluctuated with the demand for materials at the dockyard, and in 1888 it suffered from one of its occasional falls in traffic — notably, on this occasion, in armoured plate, coal and stores. Fortunately in 1889 activity increased. The Dockyard Extension was really such an asset to the dockyard that the Admiralty wanted more control over it. On 24th April, 1891 the P&T Board was told that the Admiralty had given notice of its intention to redeem the annuity of £933 7s. 10d. on Dockyard stock by the payment of a lump sum of £23,334 15s. 5d. on 1st January, 1892. The sum was actually paid in February 1892, the settlement giving the Admiralty ownership and complete responsibility for the Extension railway within the dockyard. The P&T continued to maintain and work the railway between Pembroke Dock station and the dockyard gates.

The Dockyard Extension transaction may have caused dissension amongst the P&T Directors. The evidence is lacking, but it must be said that on 5th February, 1892, J.J. Barrow resigned both as Chairman and as a Director of the company. His resignation was accepted with regret, and on the same day he transferred 5509 ordinary shares and 8440 Preference shares to his second wife. Remarkably enough, the minutes for the next meeting a fortnight later record that J.J. Barrow wished to withdraw his resignation, and so was re-elected to the Board and to the chair. Although the explanation for these odd events is not obvious, it is apparent that the Barrow family interest had not diminished at all. When J.J. Barrow was re-appointed Chairman in 1882, a son, John Burton Barrow, was a Director. Another son, Copner Walton Barrow, became a Director in 1886, and a third son, Leonard Norman Barrow, joined the Board in 1895. Although the company could hardly expand, this was really the heyday of Barrow family power; at the same period J.B. Barrow was maintaining family tradition as a Director of the Staveley Coal & Iron Co, and later L.N. Barrow also joined its Board.

In spite of the family's prosperity, the P&T still had its monetary worries. The company had to satisfy the requirements of the Regulation of Railways Act 1889, which included the provision of continuous brakes on all passenger rolling stock, and the installation of fully interlocked signalling with the block telegraph throughout. In February 1893 the Board decided to meet the cost by issuing £6000 of Debenture Stock with priority over the P&T's existing Debenture Stock. This figure had to be increased to £6,500 in June 1893, when the company approved additional expenditure on the electric train staff system as supplied by the Railway Signal Co. of Liverpool. The other signalling equipment was ordered from the Worcester firm of

Mackenzie & Holland. Several signal boxes were constructed, the largest (24 levers) being located at Tenby. The boxes at Narberth and Pembroke had 13 levers, and those at Saundersfoot, Manorbier and Pembroke Dock had 12 levers each. By June, 1894 installation of the electric train staff apparatus was under way, and the GWR agreed to contribute £40 towards the cost of instruments in their signal box at Whitland. Ground frames were provided at those places without signal boxes, and it was arranged that siding points there could be unlocked by a key on the train staff for the relevant section. At the same time small cottages were built for crossing keepers at Beavers Hill and Manorbier Newton, and ground frames were provided for the distant signals guarding the crossings. On 31st October, 1894, after four time extensions granted by the Board of Trade had expired, Mr Smedley was able to say that the work would shortly be ready for inspection. Eventually on 30th January, 1895, the Engineer told the Board that the works under the 1889 Act had been completed, adding for good measure that mixed trains were now being run in accordance with Board of Trade requirements.

In spite of these remarks, the P&T was not finished with the Regulation of Railways Act. New station accommodation was needed at Tenby and, in February 1895, the B.o.T. agreed to let the P&T issue another £1000 Debenture Stock to pay for it. In this instance the entire sum seems to have been provided by Mr Edward Davies only a few weeks after being made a Director of the company in March, 1895. The main feature of the works was improved accommodation on the up side, and the provision of a third platform. The construction of a footbridge was planned, and also improved goods facilities. Although Mr Smedley anticipated that the task would be ready for inspection in January 1896, in March of that year he could only say that the works were "nearly completed". Eventually the Board of Trade Inspector passed all the works in June 1896, suggesting a few minor additions which could be dealt with readily.

The need for improvements must have been impressed upon the company by a couple of accidents at this period. On 30th July, 1894, a goods train was derailed at Lamphey. Fortunately no one was hurt, and Mr Wood, the Engineer, estimated that the total cost of repairs would not be more than £100. The second mishap was more serious. On 12th August, 1895 a man and a horse were killed on Penally crossing. Although the coroner's verdict of accidental death attached no blame to the company's servants there was a recommendation that at busy times a P&T employee should be placed at the crossing. It is not clear if the company ever took such action, but the Board did resolve to make a £10 token payment (without liability) to the man's unfortunate widow and children. Accidents apart, there was a steady increase in traffic and train mileage at this time which increased wear and tear on the railway. Whereas in 1892 139,306 train miles were run, in 1894 the figure was 151,358 and in 1895 154,357. This growth must have been another stimulus towards capital investment.

Whilst the P&T was making improvements, ambitious eyes were studying its territory. In 1893 public notices were issued in the name of the Carmarthen, Pendine and Pembroke Railway. Although no Parliamentary Bill followed, the idea was readvertised some months later as the Carmarthen, Pembroke and South Milford Haven Railway. This scheme had echoes of the P&T's own proposals of 1866 for a railway between Carmarthen and the P&T, independent of the GWR. The main line of the CP&SMHR was to run west from the LNWR at Abergwili around Carmarthen and south towards Pendine, throwing off a short branch to Laugharne as it went. Pendine, the intended terminus of the abortive Whitland, Cronware & Pendine Railway of 1877, was the principal place on the proposed route before it joined the P&T south of Templeton. Suffice to say that the new scheme was even less successful than the WC&PR: the latter obtained an Act, but the Bill for this project was withdrawn. The P&T noted it, but made no further comment.

The next scheme was more threatening. The possibility of access to a west Wales port like Fishguard had long held attractions for the powerful LNWR. Instead of upsetting the GWR by promoting a railway of its own the LNWR took an interest in the North Pembroke & Fishguard Railway, which in 1895 sought to circumvent the Great Western by a new railway between its line and the LNWR at Abergwili. The latter company was to have running powers over the new route, which ran from Egremont south east to Narberth, Amroth and Pendine before turning north to Carmarthen and Abergwili. As originally drafted the Bill envisaged not only a new station in Carmarthen, but two connections with the P&TR near Narberth, and a new alignment for part of the existing North Pembrokeshire route. The P&T petitioned against the Bill, and the clauses concerning the junctions with that company were withdrawn. Although the Bill as a whole failed, it was reintroduced in the following year and Parliamentary powers were then obtained. By 1896, however, the antics of the NP&FR were of academic interest to the Pembroke & Tenby, because it was now clear that the P&T would become part of the Great Western. The reality of railway politics west of Carmarthen was that the GWR held the existing main line. Although little loved locally, the Great Western was practically unassailable.

It is not clear when the first discussions took place on the possible sale of the P&T to the GWR. There were certainly negotiations of some sort early in 1894 because on 1st June, 1894, the Board received a report on them from Mr Smedley. It was a mark of their confidence in the man that the Directors resolved to leave a settlement with the Great Western in his care, subject to the proviso that he obtain not less than 115% in cash or an equivalent amount in GWR stock. As a further indication of their esteem, and as a tribute to the many years he had given to the company, the Directors elected Isaac Smedley to the Board. At the next half yearly shareholders' meeting J.B. Barrow expressed the Directors' thanks for his management of the railway, and their pleasure at his having joined them on the Board.

The available P&T papers say remarkably little about the negotiations with the Great Western; throughout 1894 and 1895 they are largely preoccupied with the improvements being carried out under the Regulation of Railways Act. However, on 5th September, 1895, Smedley advised the P&T Board that the GWR had a scheme to move Carmarthen Town station to the south side of the river in order to run main line trains into and out of it, instead of setting down passengers at Carmarthen Junction as at that time. If this happened, Mr Smedley pointed out, it would be necessary to run GWR trains over the P&T loop. In that event, the Board agreed, the P&T would want to control working and participate in the traffic receipts. At this date, evidently, the Directors did not foresee the early demise of the Pembroke & Tenby Railway.

In the following summer the passing of the P&TR was both anticipated and symbolised by the death of Isaac Smedley on 12th June, 1896, aged 55. The local press described him as "generally respected" and referred to his honesty and genial disposition. At a Board meeting on 20th June attended by no less than four Barrows, the Directors expressed their sincere condolences to his family and recorded their great appreciation of his services. Rather surprisingly in view of the imminent Great Western take-over, they then agreed to advertise the vacant post of General Manager. At least eight applicants came forward, including Mr Wood, the Engineer, and John Henry, the capable station master at Pembroke Dock, but events moved rapidly and no appointment was made.

On 3rd July, 1896 an important meeting took place at Paddington. Mr A. Griffith Boscawen, M.P. a Director and Mr Moon, a barrister, represented the P&TR in discussing the lease and sale of the railway to the GWR. Various essential points were settled and it was agreed that the lease should take effect from 1st July. The terms of an agreement for the merger of the companies were also settled, to take effect a year later. When the P&T Board next met, on 3rd September, these negotiations were approved and it was resolved to seal both the lease and agreement for sale. On the same day, a dividend of 1½% was declared on Preference shares, a rather lower figure than in the

1880s and early 1890s when dividends ranged between 2% and 4¾%.

By now there was little more to be done. In September 1896 the Great Western prepared a full inventory and valuation of the P&T's equipment and stores, and later there was some debate over the apportionment of monies between the companies. According to the minute book the last P&T Board meeting was held on 29th September, 1897, at 35 Hyde Park Gardens, London. J.J. Barrow, J.B. Barrow and L.N. Barrow were present, with the Secretary, Mr Poole, in attendance. They noted that the Royal Assent had been given to the GWR (Additional Powers) Act on 6th August, causing the P&TR to become part of the Great Western from 1st July, 1897, and they gave consolidation to some financial matters. The P&T now faded away: the last shareholders meeting on 15th December, 1897, did not raise a quorum. Only L.N. Barrow was present, representing the family which was so much a part of P&T history. They continued to be involved in the M&MR until 1906, when it too was leased by the GWR. J.J. Barrow, the P&T Chairman who resigned twice, lived on until 1903.

Chapter Ten
Locomotives and Rolling Stock

Locomotives

A full account of the locomotives of the Pembroke & Tenby Railway was published in 1956 by the Railway Correspondence and Travel Society in Part 3 of their series *Locomotives of the Great Western Railway*. This is a careful and reliable study and it is not necessary to cover the same ground in such detail here. However, for the sake of completeness some mention must be made of P&T motive power.

The first locomotive to run on the P&T was David Davies' engine *Llandinam*. Named after his home village in mid-Wales, the engine was first used on the contract for the construction of the Newtown and Machynlleth Railway. In 1863 it was transferred to the P&T, and it seems to have been removed again before the contractors handed over working to the company in 1870. As a small 0–6–0 saddle tank, with cylinders measuring 11 in. x 17 in. and driving wheels of 3 ft 1½ in. diameter, it can hardly have been suited to working heavier trains. The engine was built by Manning Wardle & Co. of Leeds in 1861, works number 33, and later worked for the Carmarthenshire Iron & Coal Co.

In 1862 the contractor ordered two 2–2–2 tank locomotives from Sharp, Stewart & Co. of Manchester. According to the Sharp, Stewart order book these were completed and despatched in April 1863. Named *Tenby* and *Milford*, works numbers 1411 and 1410, they had double frames and 12 in. x 18 in. cylinders. The driving wheels were 5 ft in diameter, and the leading and trailing wheels 3 ft 6 in. The wheelbase was 12 ft 8 in. and the weight 20 tons 3½ cwt. When built they were equipped with weatherboards only; cabs were added later. In 1876 *Milford* acquired a new firebox and the cylinders were enlarged to 13 in. x 18 in. In spite of some alterations to *Tenby* in 1881, it was taken out of service in 1886 to act as a stationary boiler at Tenby workshops. *Milford* fared better, being rebuit at Tenby in January 1890. In its new condition it carried a boiler measuring 9 ft 6 in. x 3 ft 8 in. (outside) and had a firebox 3 ft long. The tank capacity was 450 gallons. *Milford* was withdrawn in June 1901, as GWR No. 1360, having ceased work some time earlier. Rather surprisingly it was not scrapped until March 1908. Sir O.H.P. Scourfield wrote of these engines that "considering their tiny proportions they were perfect marvels as regards speed and hauling power". He also recalled how, in the period between 1868 and 1872, he had seen one hold her own alongside the GWR broad gauge locomotive *Brunel* on a level stretch west of Carmarthen, and that with a relatively heavier train.

David Davies had many dealings with Sharp, Stewart & Co. on behalf of his Welsh railway concerns. In 1864 he placed at least three orders with the Manchester company. The first, order No. 480, was for four six-coupled goods engines for the M&MR, the second, No. 489, was for three similar engines for the P&T, and the third, No. 490, was for three 2–4–0 mixed passenger engines. Subsequently David Davies and the manufacturer agreed to some amendments. The eventual outcome was complex, and confounded by uncertainty as to how far Davies switched engines between the P&T and the M&M. A brief summary of the apparent results for the P&T is provided, with the important proviso that actual proof is lacking. In 1865 two locomotives were delivered to Pencader in satisfaction of order 480, these 0–6–0s being originally named *Lady Elizabeth* and *General Wood* (Sharp, Stewart works numbers 1589 and 1596). In the following year two 2–4–0s were despatched via Aberystwyth in respect of order 490, these locomotives being initially named *Pembroke* and *Owen* probably Sharp, Stewart works numbers 1712 and 1713 but possibly numbers 1712 and 1756. It is doubtful whether *Owen* reached the P&T that year. Almost certainly the third 2–4–0 (works number 1756 of 1866) supplied in 1867, never went beyond the M&M. It was given the name *Lady Elizabeth,* and the 0–6–0 of that name appears to have been given the nameplates of *Owen* instead. The 2–4–0 *Owen* became *Carmarthen,* and eventually passed into M&M ownership. The 0–6–0 *Owen* was transferred to the P&T. To complete the picture, David Davies appears to have received two engines in satisfaction of order 489, but evidently only one of these ran on the P&T. This was the 0–6–0 *Davies* (works number 1844 of 1867) which was delivered via Aberystwyth in May, 1868.

Pembroke & Tenby engines carried only names until 1872, when they were numbered in the order of their arrival on the railway. Accordingly the 2–4–0 *Pembroke* became No. 3. It had 5 ft 6 in. driving wheels and 3 ft 6 in. leading wheels. The wheelbase was 14 ft 3 in. and the cylinders 16 in. x 20 in. The total heating surface was 914.8 sq ft, and the working pressure 120 lb. The total weight of the engine was 24 tons 16 cwt. A four-wheel tender was fitted because the P&T turntables could not accommodate the locomotive with anything larger. The tender had 3 ft 6 in. wheels, and could carry 3 tons of coal and 1200 gallons of water. In 1875 *Pembroke* was fitted with a new copper firebox, and in August, 1887 both the boiler and firebox were replaced when the locomotive was rebuilt at Tenby. Thereafter the engine had a boiler pressure of 130 lb. *Pembroke* appears to have been the only one of the Sharp, Stewart engines to wander from home, because by 1899 it was to be seen in the guise of GWR No. 1361 working passenger services on the Didcot, Newbury and Southampton line. The locomotive was withdrawn in April, 1902, and scrapped two months later.

After the contractors handed over train working to the P&T the company soon realised that there was a need for more motive power. In October 1871, Isaac Smedley and his colleague Richard Metcalf attended a "jumble sale" of older engines belonging to the Llanelly Railway. It appears that they bid unsuccessfully for *Victoria*, a Beyer Peacock 0–4–2 of 1857 vintage. As most Llanelly locomotives did not enjoy a marvellous reputation, the P&T probably did well not to buy. Almost certainly the company did better by opting for a familiar Sharp, Stewart 0–6–0. In the summer of 1872 J.J. Barrow and D. Davies paid for a third locomotive of the type, which was named *Cambria* (Sharp, Stewart works number 2230).

Owen, *Davies* and *Cambria* were numbered 4, 5 and 6 on the P&TR. They were all inside framed 0–6–0s with 4ft 6in. driving wheels, a wheelbase of 14ft 9in. and cylinders measuring 16in. x 24in. As built *Owen* had a total heating surface of 951.5 sq ft, a grate area of 14.0 sq ft, and a boiler pressure of 120 lb. Originally cabless, the locomotive weighed 26 tons. *Davies* and *Cambria* were similar in all essential respects but, whereas *Owen* and *Davies* had four-wheel tenders weighing 14 tons (like that fitted to *Pembroke*), *Cambria* had a six-wheel tender weighing 19 tons. The wheels were of 3ft 6in. diameter, and the tank accommodated 1450 gallons. *Owen* was rebuilt at Tenby in August 1888, and provided with a new boiler. Numbered 1362 by the GWR, it was withdrawn in January 1899 and broken up in March, 1902. *Davies* was also reboilered when reconstructed at Tenby in January 1893, but although numbered 1363 by the Great Western it was withdrawn in May, 1899, and scrapped five months later. *Cambria* was renamed *Tenby* in 1886, on the withdrawal of the 2–2–2T *Tenby*. It was eventually rebuilt and reboilered at Tenby in January 1895, and survived in service as GWR No. 1364 until October 1903. It was broken up in the following month.

No. 7, *Holmwood*, was actually a Swindon product, designed by William Dean. An 0–6–0 side tank, it was built in September 1883, as GWR No. 1813 the first of a class which was to number forty engines. In 1883 the locomotive was purchased by Messrs Barrow and Davies on behalf of the P&T, and named after J.J. Barrow's country house near Tunbridge Wells. It had 17in. x 24in. cylinders, 4ft 6in. driving wheels and a 15ft 6in. wheelbase. The weight in working order was 39 tons 12 cwt and, with a tractive effort of 15,685 lb., *Holmwood* was soon regarded as a useful addition to stock. On its return to the Great Western *Holmwood* was renumbered 1883, but retained its name. In July 1903, after a fairly short spell as a saddle tank, it became the first of the GWR's pannier tank rebuilds. In this condition it had a weight of 44 tons 8 cwt, a boiler pressure of 165 lb., and a tractive effort of 17,525 lb. When *Holmwood* was withdrawn in July 1928 after some years of service in the Newport area, it was one of the first of the class to go to scrap.

No. 8 *Stella* was a 2–4–0 tender locomotive constructed at Swindon in December 1884. Like *Holmwood, Stella* was the first of a class and was handed over to the P&TR very soon after it was built. *Stella* had double frames, and cylinders measuring 17 in. x 26 in. The coupled wheels were 5 ft 1 in. in diameter, the leading wheels 3 ft 7 in., and the wheelbase was 17 ft. The weight in working order was 36 tons, and the tractive effort 14,658 lb. The total heating surface was 1209.86 sq ft, and the original boiler had a dome on the front ring of two. When *Stella* returned to GW ownership it completed a class of twenty-five locomotives standardised by Dean from no less than four assorted but related designs. The class now became known as the "Stella" or "3201" class — 3201 being the number allotted to *Stella* by the GWR. In 1902, however, the *Stella* nameplates were removed, and as nameless 3201 the engine underwent several boiler changes and other alterations. Although it seems that 3201 continued to do some work in South Wales prior to World War I, she was also seen in the West Midlands. When withdrawn from service in October 1933, No. 3201 was allocated to Wellington MPD, Shropshire.

In spite of extensive enquiries no documentary evidence on P&T locomotive liveries has come to light. However it is thought that the locomotives were painted green or black, the former being smartly lined out for use on passenger services. The very few photographs available seem to substantiate this belief, although it must be said that an early picture of the 2–2–2T *Tenby* depicts a cabless engine in a pale livery, with elaborate lining out in a darker shade. This may indicate either that locomotive liveries were never standardised, or that they were altered once or twice.

Early in 1886 the GWR decided to do some surreptitious research into the state of the P&T's stock. William Dean despatched Inspector Ludgate to Pembrokeshire to make discreet enquiries, and subsequently he valued the company's seven active locomotives at £14,000. Ten years later, following the take-over of the P&T, it was necessary to make a full valuation and inventory of all Pembroke & Tenby stock as at 1st July, 1896. Inspector W.H. Ludgate was responsible for this more thorough valuation, and it is rather amusing to see now how his assessment varied with that made for the P&TR. For the record the figures are set out below, together with a note of each locomotive's final P&T shed allocation.

Name	Built	P&T Valuation	GWR Valuation	1896 Shed allocation
No. 1 stationary engine(ex *Tenby*)	1863	£200	–	Tenby works
No. 2 tank engine *Milford*	1863	£800	£600	Tenby
No. 3 engine and tender*Pembroke*	1866	£1,600	£900	Whitland
No. 4 engine and tender*Owen*	1865	£1,800	£1,000	Pembroke Dock
No. 5 engine and tender*Davies*	1867	£2,000	£1,400	Tenby
No. 6 engine and tender*Tenby* (ex *Cambria*)	1872	£2,000	£1,600	Tenby
No. 7 tank engine *Holmwood*	1882	£1,600	£1,000	Pembroke Dock
No. 8 engine and tender*Stella*	1884	£2,000	£1,200	Tenby
		£11,800	£7,700	

Pembroke Dockyard Locomotives

Although no part of P&T motive power, a brief note on locomotives used at Pembroke Dockyard may be of interest. When the Admiralty took charge of railway working inside the Royal Dockyard it introduced an 0–4–0 crane tank with outside cylinders called *Blake* (Hawthorn Leslie No. 2178 of 1890). In 1901 Hawthorn Leslie supplied a similar crane tank named *Nelson* (works no. 2500), and three years later they built *Howe*, an outside-cylindered 0–4–0 saddle tank. In or after World War I *Rosyth No. 1* was brought in from Rosyth dockyard in Scotland. This was an 0–4–0ST built by A. Barclay (No. 1385 of 1914). On the closure of Pembroke dockyard in 1926 *Blake* and *Nelson* were scrapped or sold, whilst *Howe* became the property of T.W. Ward Ltd, the firm responsible for dismantling the dockyard. *Rosyth No. 1* was handed over to the Air Ministry at Pembroke Dock and, after going to RAF St Athan in 1955, was later preserved privately. The last steam locomotive said to be at the dockyard was No. 116, an 0–4–0ST by Peckett (No. 1509 of 1919). It was sold in 1961.

Carriages

In the period up to 1870 the contractors were responsible for obtaining rolling stock. The first reference in the P&T's papers occurs in August 1864, when it was stated that "the rolling stock was in thorough order, but the stock of carriages is not sufficient for the amount of traffic". Steps were soon taken to rectify the problem and, in February 1865, it was reported that more carriages were available. In fact it seems clear that the rolling stock was ordered in stages as each portion of the railway was completed. The point is confirmed by a request to Davies & Roberts on 2nd July, 1868, for a statement of rolling stock provided for the railway to Carmarthen, distinguishing between engines, carriages and trucks hired or borrowed, from those purchased by the P&TR. A similar request was made in respect of rolling stock provided for the extension between Tenby and Whitland. Although the contractors placed the orders, the P&T evidently owned some stock before July 1868.

By 1868 the passenger rolling stock seems to have been complete. It comprised no less than twenty-two four wheel vehicles, all built by the Ashbury Carriage & Wagon Co. of Manchester. Apart from two passenger brakevans, numbered 6 and 22, the carriages had oak frames and had bodies 25 ft 7 in. long, 7 ft 11 in. wide and 6 ft 3 in. high. The wheelbase was 14 ft 6 in., and vacuum and hand brakes were fitted to all except eight composite coaches, which had vacuum brakes only. Nos. 6 and 22 had oak and mahogany frames, and the bodies were 21 ft 7 in. long, 7 ft 9 in. wide and 6 ft 3 in. high. Both had a wheelbase of 12 ft and vacuum and hand brakes. The composite coaches contained four compartments, two each for first and second class, and each had gas lighting. The third class coaches were undoubtedly gloomier after dark: the five compartments had only three gaslight fittings between them! Even so, the press praised the rolling stock when the P&T opened in 1863. The carriages were described as being "very roomy and well ventilated, those of the second class being well cushioned and padded, and the third are many degrees superior to those of some other railways".

By 1894 the original third class coach No. 1 had been taken out of service, and it was replaced or rebuilt as a six-wheeled coach bearing the same number. This vehicle was constructed at the Tenby work-shops and had a body of teak and mahogany set on steel frames. Its dimensions were 27 ft 9 in. by 7 ft 11 in. by 6 ft 3 in. The wheelbase was 14 ft 6 in. and hand and vacuum brakes were fitted. The only other vehicles classified with the passenger stock were the horse-boxes, Nos. 1 and 2. The Gloucester Wagon Co. built No. 1 in 1869, and it was acquired on hire purchase under an agreement of November 1871. It measured 16 ft 3 in. long, 7 ft 10 in. wide and 7 ft 3 in. high, and had a wheelbase of 9 ft 11 in. It was equipped with hand and vacuum brakes. Horsebox No. 2, which was also four-wheeled, was built at Tenby in 1892. It was slightly smaller having a body 16 ft long, 7 ft 6 in. wide and 7 ft 2 in. high. It had oak frames and a wheelbase of 10 ft.

Inspector Ludgate's 1886 report on the P&T's stock assessed the value of the carriages as £6,900, and of the wagons as £15,075. Ten years later the figures were nothing like so impressive. By then the GWR was not prepared to put a value of more than £6,236 on the entire rolling stock. Not surprisingly this inventory of stock as at 1st July, 1896 contained more remarkable discrepancies between the valuations of the P&TR and those of the GWR. Suffice to say that the only passenger vehicle the latter regarded with any enthusiasm was the new six-wheel carriage, which they valued at £280 as against the P&TR estimate of £350. The two horseboxes also emerged with a little credit, but the Great Western's opinion of the rest was demonstrated by its rapid withdrawal. The composite coaches were taken out of service immediately, and the passenger brakevans lasted only until September 1897. Three months later all the third and brake third coaches were withdrawn with the sole exception of the new No. 1. This was destined to last another thirty years, being withdrawn eventually in June 1928.

The P&T's passenger rolling stock may be summarised as follows:

P&TR Nos	Type & Accommodation	GWR Nos.
1–3,14–16,19–21	5 compt 3rd	3990,3991,3993–5, 3998–4000
4,5,8–13	compo. 2 1st/2 2nd	–
6,22	passenger brake: luggage/guard	819,820
7	brake 3rd: 4 compt/guard	3992
17,18	brake 3rd: 2 compt/luggage/guard	3996,3997
1	5 compts 3rd	3989

Wagons

For a small railway the Pembroke & Tenby had quite a considerable fleet of freight stock, the total of 199 vehicles including two brakevans and a travelling crane. A number were built by the Ashbury Carriage & Wagon Co. and were probably obtained by the contractors. Most were built by the Gloucester Wagon Co. and acquired on hire purchase; until payment was complete they had to carry a plate acknowledging the Gloucester Wagon Co. to be the owners. Thirty wagons constructed by the Bristol Wagon Co. were obtained on a similar basis. Two timber wagons, ordered on 30th November, 1876, appear to have been the last vehicles provided by an outside manufacturer. In later years at least eighteen of the low sided wagons were regarded as engineers' ballast wagons. It is known that forty-one of the deep-sided wagons had tip ends, but the wagons so fitted have not been positively identified. The only wagons to impress the GWR in 1896 were the ten covered vans, but even they were valued at £40 each, as against the P&T assessment of £75 each. It is thought that most of the freight stock was scrapped or sold soon after acquisition by the Great Western.

At least three businesses served by the P&TR had private owner wagons and there were probably others. The official photographs of the Gloucester Railway Carriage & Wagon Co. show that in September 1902, Thomas Rees Saunders, coal merchant of Pembroke, was supplied with a seven-plank 10 ton open wagon which was numbered 6. It was painted black with white lettering. In March 1903, William Thomas, coal, lime and manure merchant of Whitland, obtained a five plank 10 ton open wagon, No. 3. This was painted the colour of lead, and the letters were white shaded in black. Meanwhile in 1900 it is known that the Bonville's Court Coal Co. of Saundersfoot had fifteen standard gauge private owner wagons. Some of these were almost certainly in service during the independent days of the P&TR.

The livery of Pembroke & Tenby rolling stock is a topic open to some debate. The carriages are believed to have been brown, but the exact shade is not known. Amongst the wagons there was some variety, because to judge from the builders' official photographs most had dark paintwork. Open wagon No. 54 was an exception being finished in a pale colour, with black lettering. The only other evidence is provided by an 1896 list of paints held by the Carriage & Wagon department, but unfortunately it does not say when or how the paints were used. For the record (for what it is worth!) the largest quantities of paint in stock were purple-brown, amber, black, red lead and white lead. Oak and body varnish was available in quantity, as was Oxford Ochre and Japan Gold — the latter perhaps for use in lining and lettering. All in all, as P&T trains were a familiar sight for over thirty years, it is strange that no better references to their colours have so far come to light.

Summary Table
Wagons (including goods brakevans and travelling crane)

P&TR Nos.	Type and Load Weight	Length	Breadth	Height	Wheelbase	Builder
1	Goods brakevan	17' 5"	× 6' 8"	× 6' 2"	9' 11"	Gloucester Wagon Co.
2	Goods brakevan	17' 5"	× 6' 3"	× 6' 2"	10' 7"	Gloucester Wagon Co.
1,2,4–6,8–18 27–36,103–106	7 ton low-sided	15' 0"	× 7' 0"	× 1' 6"	9' 0"	Ashbury
3,7	6 ton timber	12' 1"	× 6' 11"	× 3' 0"	7' 6"	Ashbury
93–96		12' 0"	× 6' 8"	× 3' 0"	7' 6"	Gloucester
19–26	7 ton low-sided coal	15' 0"	× 6' 11"	× 2' 6"	9' 0"	Ashbury
101,102	7 ton low-sided coal	14' 5"	× 6' 8"	× 3' 0"	8' 3"	Gloucester
37–66	7 ton deep sided	13' 6"	× 6' 8"	× 2' 10"	8' 3"	Gloucester
67–86	7 ton deep sided	15' 0"	× 6' 8"	× 2' 3"	9' 2"	Gloucester
111–113	7 ton deep sided	13' 6"	× 6' 8"	× 2' 3"	9' 2"	Gloucester
114–135	7 ton deep sided	14' 5"	× 7' 0"	× 2' 10"	8' 3"	Gloucester
136–165	7 ton deep sided	13' 6"	× 6' 9"	× 2' 3"	9' 2"	Bristol
166–195	7 ton deep sided	14' 6"	× 6' 9"	× 2' 11"	8' 3"	Gloucester
196	10 ton deep sided	14' 8"	× 6' 9"	× 3' 8"	8' 6"	Birmingham
87–92	8 ton covered van	14' 8"	× 6' 9"	× 6' 0"	9' 3"	Gloucester
107–110	8 ton covered van	14' 8"	× 6' 9"	× 6' 0"	9' 3"	Ashbury
97–100	8 ton cattle wagon	15' 6"	× 7' 3"	× 6' 6"	9' 3"	Gloucester
1	Travelling crane (lifting up to 7 tons)	17' 0"	× 7' 6"		11' 0"	Ellis & Co., Manchester

N.B.
There were some differences in detail dimensions amongst wagons of the same type. The figures given represent the usual position.

Chapter Eleven
Under the Great Western

In spite of the sums spent on improvements during the early 1890s, the GWR was not impressed by the condition of the Pembroke & Tenby Railway at the time of takeover. Most of the rolling stock was withdrawn within two or three years, and all the locomotives (except the two built at Swindon) soon went for scrap. In 1898 the Great Western decided to spend £44,000 on modernising the line, and one of the first tasks was relaying the railway from end to end. As this work took place there appears to have been some slight realignment of track: the gradient profile after reconstruction differed in some detail from that recorded earlier. By the turn of the century other improvements were in hand. The main building at Pembroke Dock acquired a canopy in 1902, and in the same year the north platform was extended and more sidings were installed to provide for increased goods and passenger traffic. The locomotive shed was also enlarged, and a new 55 ft turntable was located on the opposite side of the running lines, set alongside a coal stage and ramp. As a result of these changes the Pembroke Dock signal box was replaced in 1902 by a timber box with a 33 lever frame. At the same period it is believed that some improvements were made in accommodation at Pembroke and Manorbier. At Tenby, however, the locomotive works were closed down, and the engine shed reduced in status. Alterations at Tenby station included the closure of a public footpath across the tracks at the north end, and the provision of a new footpath from the station yard to the main road passing under the viaduct.

Improvements were also made at Whitland and Carmarthen. The P&T's engine shed at Whitland was destroyed by fire in 1901, but it was replaced (in part) in 1902 by a shed which formerly stood at Letterston on the North Pembroke & Fishguard Railway. At Carmarthen the GWR took action on a long contemplated scheme for the rebuilding of Carmarthen Town station on a much larger site south of the river. The plan involved the reconstruction of the P&T loop to provide a triangle, thereby enabling main line services to use the Town station with only one reversal. The new red brick station comprised three through platforms and two bays; both the station and the relaid P&T loop were opened to passenger traffic on 1st July, 1902. Soon after the GWR decided to replace a two road locomotive shed near the old C&C station with a new red, brick built depot and repair shop adjacent to the new Town station. This shed was brought into use on 11th February, 1907; it has been said that some of its original equipment came from the closed P&T workshops at Tenby.

In June, 1905 a summer railmotor service was inaugurated between Pembroke Dock and Saundersfoot with two daily trips over the whole

80

2–2–2T locomotive *Tenby*   *Locomotive Magazine*

2–2–2T locomotive *Milford c.* 1889/90.   *L.G.R.P., Courtesy David & Charles*

0–6–0 locomotive *Owen* at Tenby.   *Real Photographs*

0–6–0 locomotive *Tenby*.   *Real Photographs*

Locomotive *Holmwood* rebuilt by the GWR as a pannier tank and numbered 1813.
Real Photographs

GWR 3201 locomotive *Stella* before reboilering. *E. Ponteau/J.K. Reed Collection*

P&TR passenger coach No. 1, as built at Tenby, 1894. *Tenby Museum*

2–4–0 locomotive *Pembroke* running as GWR No. 1361.
L.G.R.P., Courtesy David & Charles

Rebuilt 2–4–0 locomotive No. 3201 *Stella*. *Real Photographs*

Last survivor of the Pembroke Dockyard locomotives: 0–4–0ST *Rosyth No. 1* at Briton Ferry, 3rd August, 1986. *M.R.C. Price*

P & TR van No. 87.   *Courtesy the Gloucester C & W Co.*

P & TR cattle wagon No. 99.   *Courtesy the Gloucester C & W Co.*

P & TR timber wagon No. 94.   *Courtesy the Gloucester C & W Co.*

P & TR wagon No. 54.   *Courtesy the Gloucester C & W Co.*

P&TR goods brakevan No. 1. *Courtesy the Gloucester C&W Co.*

Private owner wagon: Thomas Rees Saunders coal wagon No. 6.
Courtesy the Gloucester C&W Co.

WHITLAND, TENBY AND PEMBROKE DOCK.

Down Trains.		Week Days.								Sundays		Up Trains.		Week Days.							Sundys.	
		a.m.	a.m.	a.m.	p.m.	p.m.	p.m.	p.m.	p.m.	p.m	p m			a.m.	a.m.	a.m.	p.m.	p m	p.m	p.m	Sundys.	
Whitland ... dep		5 55		10 45	12 15	2 10	4 54	5 20	7 50		7 35	Pembroke D k dep		7 40	9 25	10 30	12 20	2 15	4 0	6 15	7 35	3 0
Narberth		6 5		10 55	12 25	2 22		5 31	8 0		7 46	Pembroke		7 44	9 33	10 35	12 25	2 20	4 5	6 25	7 42	3 5
Kilgetty		6 22		11 11	12 41	2 36		5 44	8 16		7 59	Lamphey		7 49		10 41	12 40	2 26	4 10	6 18	7 48	3 10
Saundersfoot		6 24		11 14	12 44	2 39	5 26	5 47	8 19	3 55	8 1	Manorbier		7 57	9 45	10 49	12 48	2 34	4 18	6 1s	7 48	3 18
Tenby { arr		6 35		11 25	12 55	2 50	5 40	6 0	8 35	4 5	8 15	Penally		8 4		10 56	12 56	2 41	4 25	6 25	7 53	3 25
{ dep		6 40	9 15	11 30	1 0	2 55	5 45	6 5	8 40		8 20	Tenby { arr		8 8	9 57	11 0	1 0	2 45	4 30	6 30	3	3 30
Penally		6 45	9 18	11 36	1 5	3 0		6 9	8 44		8 25	{ dep		8 10	10 5	11 6	1 8	2 50	4 35	6 35		6 39
Manorbier		6 52	9 25	11 44	1 13	3 7	5 55	6 17	8 52		8 33	Saundersfoot		8 22	10 15	11 18	1 15	3 3	4 47	6 45		3 45
Lamphey		6 59	9 33	11 51	1 21	3 17		6 26	8 59		8 40	Kilgetty		8 24		11 24	1 20	3 8	4 52	6 50		6 46
Pembroke		7 3	9 35	11 55	1 25	3 20	6 6	6 30	9 3		8 44	Narberth		8 41	10 31	11 39	1 33	3 23	5 7	7 3		7 0
Pembroke D'k arr		7 10	9 40	12 5	1 33	3 28	6 15	6 40	9 10		8 50	Whitland arr		8 52		11 55	1 45	3 35	5 20	7 15		7 10

TEMPLETON PLATFORM.—The 5.55 a.m. Train from Whitland calls at Templeton Platform on Fridays, when Market Tickets are issued to Pembroke Dock. Also the same Train calls on Saturdays, when Market Tickets are issued to Tenby and to Pembroke. For Fares and Return arrangements see Market Ticket Bills. Ordinary Tickets are also issued by the Trains which call.

Timetable of 1902

WHITLAND, TENBY AND PEMBROKE DOCK.

			Week Days.																	Sundays.		
		a.m.	a.m.	a.m.	a.m.	a.m.	p.m.	a.m.	p.m.	p.m.	p.m.	p.m.		p.m.	p.m.	p.m.	p.m.	p.m.		p.m.	p.m.	p.m.
Whitland ..... dep			5 55			10 40		11 55		2 22				5 38	5 50		7 50			10 55		7 35
Narberth			6 5	M	M	10 50	M	12 8	M	2 32				5 50	6 0	M	8 0			11 5		7 45
Templeton			6 14			11 0		12 9		2 45				6 10	6 11		8 9			11 12		7 54
Kilgetty			6 21			11 7		12 26		2 52				6 10	6 13		8 16			11 15		8 1
Saundersfoot			6 24			11 10		12 30	2 23	2 54		5 17		6 13	6 31		8 19			11 15	3 55	8 4
Tenby { arr		3rd class only	6 35			11 22		12 43	2 33	3 8		5 25		6 25	6 35		8 30			11 25	4 5	8 15
{ dep			6 40	9 10	10 55	11 25	12 22	12 50	2 36	3 12	4 20	5 30		6 40	7 0	8 32	10 15					8 20
Penally			6 45	9 12	10 59	11 31	12 26	12 53	2 39	3 18	4 24	5 33		6 43	7 9	8 35	10 15					8 25
Lydstep Halt				9 16	11 3		12 30		2 43		4 28				7 13							
Manorbier			6 52	9 21	11 8	11 39	12 34	1 2	2 48	3 25	4 32	5 41		6 51	7 19	8 43	7 25					8 36
Beavers Hill Halt				9 24	11 11		12 39		2 51		4 37				7 24							
Lamphey			6 59	9 30	11 17	11 46	12 45	1 9	2 57	3 35	4 43			6 58	7 29	8 50	10 32					8 43
Pembroke		6 20	7 3	9 37	11 22	11 50	12 50	1 13	3 2	3 38	4 48	5 51		7 2	7 34	8 53	10 35					8 47
Llanion Halt				9 42	11 27		12 55		3 7		4 53				7 39							
Pembroke Dock arr		6 20	7 10	9 43	11 28		12 0	12 56	1 20	3 8	3 45	4 54	6 0		7 10	7 40	9 0	10 40				8 55

									M					M				M		id		
		a.m.	a.m.		a.m.	a.m.		a.m.	p.m.	p.m.		p.m.	p.m.	p.m.	p.m.	p.m.	p.m.	p.m.		p.m.	p.m.	
Pembroke Dock dep		7 35	9 25			9 52		10 15	11 38	12 15	1 30	2 5	3 24	3 50	5 18	6 0	8 0	9 56		3 0		
Llanion Halt						9 53			11 39		1 31		3 29		5 19		8 1					
Pembroke		7 39	9 30			9 59		10 20	11 45	12 20	1 37	2 9	3 35	3 54	5 25	6 5	8 7	9 35		3 5		
Lamphey		7 44				10 3		10 26	11 53	12 25	1 41	2 14	3 43	3 59	5 31	6 10	8 12	9 39		3 10		
Beavers Hill Halt						10 9			11 59		1 47		3 49		5 37		8 17					
Manorbier		7 52	9 45			10 13		10 34	12 3	12 32	1 51	2 22	3 53	4 7	5 40	6 18	8 21	9 47		3 13		
Lydstep Halt						10 17			12 7		1 55		3 57		5 46		8 25					
Penally		7 59	9 52			10 21		10 41	12 11	12 41	1 59	2 29	4 1	4 13	5 50	6 27	9 7	9 55		3 25		
Tenby { arr		8 3	9 57			10 26		10 46	12 16	12 45	2 4	2 30	4 6	4 19	5 55	6 31	8 34	9 58		3 30		
{ dep		8 21	10 15					10 50		12 50		2 6	2 35		4 25		6 35			10 15	3 35	6 30
Saundersfoot		8 26						11 5			1 5		2 58		4 40		6 49			10 26	3 45	6 40
Kilgetty		8 33						11 13			1 5		3 6		4 47		6 56			10 29		6 45
Templeton								11 20			1 15		3 15		4 56		7 5			10 37		6 51
Narberth		8 42						11 29			1 24		3 24		5 10		7 17			10 47		7 1
Whitland arr		8 55						11 42			1 35		3 24		5 10		7 17			10 47		7 12

September 1908 Timetable.

WHITLAND, TENBY, and PEMBROKE.—Great Western.

Miles	Down. Paddington Station.	Week Days mrn	Sleeping Car, (1 cl.) London to Pembroke Dock. aft	mrn	mrn	aft (Saturdays only.)	non	mrn	aft (Except Saturdays.)	mrn	aft	Suns.
	60 London ....dep.	3 cl.	9 15	....	1a0	3 cl.	....	8d45	3 cl.	1130	....	
—	Whitland ....dep.	....	5 55	....	1040		12 0	2 30		5 26	7 55	
5¼	Narberth	....	6 5	....	1052		1215	2 41		5 37	8 5	
8¼	Templeton	....	6 14	....	11 1		1225	2 50		5 46	8 15	
10¾	Kilgetty	....	6 21	....	11 8		1232	2 57		5 53	8 23	
11¾	Saundersfoot	....	6 24	....	1114		1236	3 3		5 58	8 27	
15¾	Tenby .... arr.	....	6 35	....	1122		1248	3 11		6 5	8 35	
	Tenby .... dep	....	6 40	9 22	1128		1255	3 18		6 10	8 40	
17	Penally	....	6 45	9 26	1132		1258	3 23		6 14	8 44	
20¼	Manorbier	....	6 52	9 36	1141		1 7	3 34		6 21	8 52	
23¼	Lamphey	....	6 59	9 43	1147		1 14	3 42		6 30	....	
25¼	Pembroke	6 24	7 3	9 47	1153	1 0	1 18	3 51	5 40	6 35	9 3	
—	Golden Hill Platform..	6 27	....	9 50	1156	1 3	1 23	3 53	5 42	6 38	....	
27¼	Pembroke Dock.... arr.	6 31	7 10	9 54	12 0	1 7	1 27	3 57	5 46	6 42	9 8	

Miles	Up.	Week Days mrn	Through Carriages, Pembroke Dock to London. mrn	aft	aft (Saturdays only.)	aft	aft	aft (Except Saturdays.)	Sleeping Car, Whitland to London. aft	aft	Suns.
—	Pembroke Dock....dep	7 45	1020	1215	1235	2 5	3 40	5 30	6 0	7 30	
—	Golden Hill Platform..	....	1025	1220	1240	2 10	3 45	5 34	....	....	
2	Pembroke	7 50	1029	1224	1242	2 17	3 48	5 36	6 5	7 37	
3½	Lamphey	7 54	1033	1228	3 cl.	2 21	3 53	3 cl.	6 10	....	
7	Manorbier	8 2	1042	1236		2 29	4 2		6 18	7 49	
10¼	Penally	8 10	1049	1244		2 37	4 10		6 27	7 57	
11½	Tenby .... arr.	8 13	1052	1247		2 40	4 13		6 31	8 0	
	Tenby .... dep.	8 16	1058	1255		2 47	4 18		6 35	....	
15¾	Saundersfoot	8 27	1111	1 9		3 1	4 30		6 45	....	
16¾	Kilgetty	8 31	1115	1 13		3 5	4 34		6 49	....	
19	Templeton	8 38	1122	1 20		3 12	4 41		6 56	....	
22	Narberth	8 48	1132	1 30		3 21	4 55		7 5	....	
27¼	Whitland 60, 64 ... arr.	8 58	1142	1 40		3 30	5 5		7 17	....	
261	64 London (Pad.) arr.	4 20	6 10	....	....	9 35	....	....	3 30	....	

a Except Mondays. d By Slip carriage.

Timetable of October 1911.

Bradshaw timetable of 1930.

WHITLAND, TENBY, and PEMBROKE DOCK.

Miles	Down.	Week Days aft	mrn	mrn	aft S	nn Z	aft	mrn Z	aft	Sundays.
	Paddington, 64 London.....dep.	925	1255 M	1255	..	855	..	1155	1 55	..
—	Whitland ......dep.	535	8 15	1030	..	219	..	5 30	8 0	..
5½	Narberth	547	8 26	1042	..	230	..	5 42	8 12	..
8½	Templeton	556	8 35	1052	..	239	..	5 50	8 21	..
10½	Kilgetty	6 2	8 41	1058	..	245	..	5 56	8 27	..
11½	Saundersfoot	6 6	8 50	11 2	..	250	..	6 1	8 31	..
15¼	Tenby .... arr.	614	8 58	1110	..	258	..	6 9	8 39	..
	Tenby .... dep.	618	9 0	1125	1 45	3 1	5 45	6 13	8 43	..
17	Penally ¶	622	9 4	1129	1 49	3 5	5 49	6 17	8 48	..
20½	Manorbier ¶	630	9 14	1139	2 0	313	5 59	6 25	8 56	..
23¼	Lamphey	636	9 22	1145	2 8	319	6 7	6 31	9 2	..
25½	Pembroke	641	9 26	1150	2 16	324	6 11	6 35	9 7	..
25¾	Golden Hill Plat. ..	..	9 29	..	..	..	6 14	..	..	..
27¼	Pembroke Dock arr.	647	9 33	1155	2 21	330	6 18	6 43	9 12	..

Miles	Up.	Week Days mrn Z	mrn Z	aft S	aft	aft	aft	aft	aft	Sundays.
—	Pembroke Dock dep.	8 5	1050	1 0	2 5	3 55	5 0	6 25	8 10	..
1½	Golden Hill Plat. ..	..	..	1 5	..	..	5 5	..	..	..
2	Pembroke	8 11	1057	1 8	2 13	4 5	5 8	6 34	8 16	..
3½	Lamphey ¶	8 15	11 1	1 12	2 17	4 9	5 12	6 38	8 20	..
7	Manorbier ¶	8 23	11 9	1 20	2 25	4 17	5 20	6 46	8 28	..
10¼	Penally	8 30	1119	1 30	2 34	4 27	5 30	6 53	8 35	..
11½	Tenby .... arr.	8 33	1122	1 33	2 37	4 30	5 33	6 56	8 38	..
	Tenby .... dep.	8 39	1127	..	2 39	4 32	..	7 0	8 40	..
15¾	Saundersfoot	8 51	1139	..	2 51	4 43	..	7 12	8 51	..
16¾	Kilgetty	8 55	1143	..	2 55	4 47	..	7 16	8 55	..
19	Templeton	9 2	1150	..	3 3	4 54	..	7 23	9 2	..
22	Narberth...[& below	9 11	1159	..	3 13	5 3	..	7 33	9 11	..
27¼	Whitland 64, 69, arr	9 20	12 8	..	3 22	5 12	..	7 42	9 20	..
261	69 London (P.) arr.	3 10	6 10	..	9 40	..	..	3 25	..	..

M Monday morns only. S Sats. only. Z Thro Carriages between London (Pad.) and Pembroke Dock.
¶ "Halt" at Lydstep between Penally and Manorbier and at Beavers Hill, between Manorbier and Lamphey.

WHITLAND, TENBY AND PEMBROKE DOCK.

Week Days only.

		a.m.	a.m.	noon	p.m.	p.m.		p.m.				a.m.		a.m.		p.m.	p.m.		p.m.
Whitland	dep.	6 50	11 0	...	3 23	7 0	...	9 30	Pembroke Dock	...dep.	7 35	...	11 25	...	2 5	3 55	...	6 20
Narberth	„	7 3	11 12	...	3 35	7 12	...	9 42	Pembroke	„	7 45	...	11 32	.	2 13	4 3	...	6 28
Templeton	„	7 12	11 22	...	3 44	7 22	...	9 51	Lamphey	„	7 49	...	11 36	...	2 17	4 7	...	6 32
Kilgetty	„	7 18	11 28	...	3 50	7 28	...	9 57	Beavers Hill Halt	„		...		...		4 12	...	
Saundersfoot	„	7 23	11 32	...	3 53	7 32	...	10 1	Manorbier	„	8 1	...	11 44	...	2 25	4 17	...	6 41
Tenby	{ arr.	7 31	11 40		4 1	7 40	...	10 9	Lydstep Halt	„		...	11 48	...	2 29	4 21	...	.
	{ dep.	7 36		12 0	4 5	7 45	...	10 12	Penally	„	8 7	...	11 53	...	2 34	4 26	...	6 47
Penally	„	7 40	.	12 4	4 9	7 49	...	10 17	Tenby	{ arr.	8 10	...	11 56	...	2 37	4 29	...	6 50
Lydstep Halt	„		.	12 8	.		...			{ dep.	8 15	...	12 0	...	2 40	4 33	...	6 55
Manorbier	„	7 57	.	12 15	4 18	7 59	...	10 25	Saundersfoot	„	8 26	...	12 11	...	2 52	4 44	.	7 7
Beavers Hill Halt	„		.	12F17	.		...		Kilgetty	„	8 30	...	12 15	...	2 56	4 49	.	7 11
Lamphey	„	8 3	.	12 21	4 24	8 5	...	10 35	Templeton	„	8 37	...	12 22	...	3 3	4 56	.	7 21
Pembroke	„	8 10	.	12 27	4 30	8 13	...	10 40	Narberth	„	8 46	...	12 31	...	3 13	5 5	.	7 31
Pembroke Dock	arr.	8 15	.	12 32	4 35	8 18	...	10 45	Whitland	arr.	8 55	...	12 40	...	3 22	5 14	.	7 40

WHITLAND AND CARDIGAN.

Week Days only.

		a.m.			p.m.		.	p.m.			a.m.			a.m.			p.m.	
Whitland	dep.	6 40	...	...	4 5	...	.	7 30	Cardigan (for Gwbert-on-Sea)	dep.	7 10	...	.	11 5	...	.	6 0	.
Llanfalteg	„	6 51	...	...	4 14	...	.	7 40	Kilgerran	„	7 19	...	.	11 13	...	.	6 9	.
Login	„	7 0	...	...	4 23	...	.	7 49	Boncath	„	7 34	...	.	11 24	...	.	6 21	.
Llanglydwen	„	7 10	...	...	4 33	...	.	7 59	Crymmych Arms	„	7 48	...	.	11 37	...	.	6 35	.
Rhydowen	„	7 18	...	...	4 38	...	.	8 5	Glogue	„	7 57	...	.	11 46	...	.	6 44	.
Llanfyrnach	„	7 25	...	...	4 47	...	.	8 14	Llanfyrnach	„	8 3	...	.	11 52	...	.	6 50	.
Glogue	„	7 32	...	...	4 54	...	.	8 21	Rhydowen	„	8 11	...	.	11 59	...	.	6 58	.
Crymmych Arms	„	7 49	...	...	5 2	...	.	8 28	Llanglydwen	„	8 17	...	.	12 6	...	.	7 4	.
Boncath	„	8 5	...	...	5 15	...	.	8 41	Login	„	8 27	...	.	12 16	...	.	7 14	.
Kilgerran	„	8 15	...	...	5 25	...	.	8 51	Llanfalteg	„	8 36	...	.	12 25	...	.	7 23	.
Cardigan (for Gwbert-on-Sea)	arr.	8 22	...	.	5 32	...	.	8 58	Whitland	arr.	8 45	...	.	12 35	...	.	7 32	.

Timetable of April 1944.

Timetable of October 1947.

WHITLAND, TENBY AND PEMBROKE DOCK.

		Week Days.						Suns.				Week Days.					Suns.
							W							M		W	
		a.m.	a.m.		p.m.	p.m.	p.m.	p.m.	a.m.		p.m.	p.m.	Pembroke D'k dep.	a.m. a.m. a.m.		p.m p.m	p.m p.m	p.m.
Whitland	dep.	6 10	11 0	...	3 2	6 30	9 1	10 11	6 5	Pembroke D'k	dep.	7 45 10 31 11 40	...	1 45 3 55	6 20 8 20	...	5 55
Narberth	„	6 24	11 12	...	3 14	6 42	9 1	10 11	6 16	Pembroke	„	7 52 10 38 11 47	...	1 53 4 4	6 28 8 28	...	6 2
Templeton	„	6 30	11 22	...	3 23	6 52	9 11	10 22	6 25	Lamphey	„	7 56 10 52 11 51	...	1 57 4 9	6 32 8 32	...	6 6
Kilgetty	„	6 36	11 28	...	3 29	6 59	9 17	10 25	6 31	Beavers Hill Halt	„		...	4 14		...	
Saundersfoot	„	6 39	11 31	...	3 32	7 6	9 20	10 29	6 34	Manorbier	„	8 5 10 4 ...	...	2 5 4 17	6 41 8 38	...	6 14
Tenby	{ arr.	6 47	11 39	...	3 40	7 14	9 28	10 37	6 42	Lydstep Halt	„		...			...	
	{ dep.	6 52	11 43	...	3 44	7 18	9 31	10 40	6 45	Penally	„	8 11 10 51 12 8	...	2 14 4 26	6 47 8 44	...	6 20
Penally	„	6 56	11 47	...	3 48	7 22	9 35	10 44	6 49	Tenby	{ arr.	8 14 10 54 12 11	...	2 17 4 29	6 50 8 47	...	6 23
Lydstep Halt	„			...							{ dep.	8 17 10 57 12 15	...	2 20 4 33	6 55 8 49	...	6 25
Manorbier	„	7 4	11 55	...	3 56	7 31	9 43	10 52	6 57	Saundersfoot	„	8 25 11 2 12 23	...	2 31 4 44	7 7 9 0	...	6 36
Beavers Hill Halt	„		12F2	...						Kilgetty	„	8 32 11 11 12 30	...	2 35 4 48	7 11 9 4	...	6 40
Lamphey	„	7 10	12 6	...	4 2	7 37	9 49	11 0	7 3	Templeton	„	8 39 11 17 12 37	...	2 42 4 55	7 18 9 13	...	6 47
Pembroke	„	7 15	12 12	...	4 10	7 42	9 54	11 5	7 8	Narberth	„	8 48 11 26 12 46	...	2 51 5 4	7 28 9 21	...	6 56
Pembroke D'k	arr.	7 20	12 17	...	4 15	7 47	9 59	11 10	7 13	Whitland	arr.	8 57 11 35 12 55	...	3 0 5 13	7 37 9 36	...	7 5

WHITLAND AND CARDIGAN. (Week Days only.)

		a.m.		a.m.	p.m.		p.m.			a.m.		a.m.	a.m.		p.m.
Whitland	dep.	6 30	...	11 25	...	4 0	...	6 25	Cardigan (for Gwbert-on-Sea)	dep.	7 0	9M50	10T45	...	5 50
Llanfalteg	„	6 41	...	11 36	...	4 10	...	6 36	Kilgerran	„	7 9	9M59	10T54	...	5 59
Login	„	6 51	...	11 46	...	4 20	...	6 46	Boncath	„	7 24	10M14	11T 9	...	6 14
Llanglydwen	„	7 3	...	11 57	...	4 32	...	7 1	Crymmych Arms	„	7 37	10M27	11T22	...	6 27
Rhydowen	„	7 9	...	12 3	...	4 38	...	7 7	Glogue	„	7 48	10M38	11T33	...	6 38
Llanfyrnach	„	7 18	...	12 12	...	4 46	...	7 16	Llanfyrnach	„	7 55	10M44	11T40	...	6 45
Glogue	„	7 27	...	12 20	...	4 54	...	7 24	Rhydowen	„	8 4	10M53	11T49	...	6 54
Crymmych Arms	„	7 39	...	12 30	...	5 4	...	7 34	Llanglydwen	„	8 11	11M 0	11T53	...	7 0
Boncath	„	7 52	...	12 43	...	5 17	...	7 47	Login	„	8 22	11M11	12T 9	...	7 12
Kilgerran	„	8 2	...	12 53	...	5 27	...	7 57	Llanfalteg	„	8 33	11M21	12T19	...	7 22
Cardigan (for Gwbert-on-Sea)	arr.	8 11	...	1 2	...	5 36	...	8 6	Whitland	arr.	8 43	11M31	12T29	...	7 32

D—Calls to pick up or set down passengers. Passengers wishing to alight must give notice to the Guard at the previous stopping station, and those desiring to join should give the necessary hand signal to the Driver.
F—Fridays only.
G—Saturdays excepted.
M—Mondays, Fridays and Saturdays only.

S—Saturdays only.
T—Tuesdays, Wednesdays and Thursdays only.
W—Mondays, Wednesdays and Fridays only.
Z—Through Train from (or to) London (Paddington).
‡—Adjoins Pembrey and Burry Port Station.
¶—For Tumble.

branch. Halts were opened at Llanion, a mere 21 chains from Pembroke Dock, at Beavers Hill near Manorbier, and at Lydstep. The latter was not new of course,but provided with a regular service for the first time. The halt at Llanion was not a success, and after the summer of 1908 it was deleted from the timetable. Instead, on 1st July, 1909 a new halt was opened at Golden Hill, near the southern end of the tunnel between Pembroke and Pembroke Dock. Apart from Golden Hill the halts were used only in July, August and September when fairly frequent railmotor services were operating west of Tenby; according to one report in 1907 a railmotor also worked once a day to Fishguard and back. Although the railmotors were small, weighing about 32 tons, it was not uncommon to see them running with a van attached. Steam railmotors appearing on the P & T route at different periods to World War I included numbers 3, 8, 13, 14, 17, 33, 37, 48, 55, 57, 63, 68, 71, 77 and 83.

In July 1897, the month the GWR assumed ownership of the P & T, the passenger timetable showed seven trains in each direction, one of which ran only from Pembroke Dock to Tenby and back. There was also one train each way over the whole line on Sundays. By April, 1910 the timetable advertised ten trains travelling in the up direction and nine down, although two in each direction were third class only services between Pembroke Dock and Pembroke intended primarily for dockyard workmen. The 10.15 am from Pembroke Dock conveyed through coaches for Paddington from Tenby, and it is believed that through coaches in the down direction were attached to the train leaving Whitland at 5.25 pm. In addition a sleeping car from London was attached to the 5.55 am train from Whitland, and this returned as part of the 6.00 pm from Pembroke Dock. The timetable included one local train in each direction between Tenby and Pembroke Dock only, but there was one Sunday train each way over the whole line between May and November.

Prior to 1914 there were usually three freight trains a day each way over the P & T line, and additional trains were run as required to serve the busier stations. For many years heavy traffic for Pembroke Dockyard was a feature of the P & T route, the freight including armour plate, ship materials and coal. The movement of troops and stores to the garrison at Pembroke Dock and other camps nearby was another familiar sight, and in the early years of the twentieth century military traffic developed steadily. Soon after the formation of the Territorial Army in 1908 railwaymen became accustomed to the "territorial camp season", as trains brought territorials to south Pembrokeshire for training. Penally was a common destination for these men, although the lack of a loop at the station did present an operating problem. During the season it became usual to permit empty carriage stock to be propelled from Penally to Tenby Lower Yard for stabling; remarkable as it may seem nowadays, such carriage stock sometimes remained in the sidings unused throughout the duration of a camp.

Agricultural traffic was important at almost all the stations along the line. Pembroke was the setting for some big horse fairs, and the traffic was so considerable that cattle wagons were frequently provided in place of horse boxes. On fair days Pembroke must have resembled a town in the American West, as animals were driven along the roads between the station and the sales ground. Narberth, too, had its horse sales and monthly agricultural fairs, and the scene there could be one of bustling activity as livestock, drovers and dealers mixed with school children and other regular passengers as they passed to and fro between station and town by coach, cart or on foot. A cheese and butter factory added another dimension to the Narberth picture, and milk traffic was flourishing. By now, indeed, liquid milk was being moved in increasing quantities over the P&T line to dairies at Whitland, Carmarthen and elsewhere. The setting up of dairies at Whitland in about 1910 gave the business a boost. Potatoes and rabbits at Pembroke, sand at Manorbier and more rabbits from stations north of Tenby were other kinds of agricultural freight. Prior to World War I there was still trade in lime and limestone from Black Rock quarries, Tenby, and at Saundersfoot anthracite was the main traffic. Substantial quantities were sent to brewers and maltsters at Burton-on-Trent, and in South East England, and consignments also went to Cornwall for use in the tin industry.

By 1914 much of the P&T had been modernised to Great Western standards, and apart from the buildings, relics of the company were few. The strongest links with the P&T's independent days were provided by the several P&T officials who remained in railway service. John Henry was station master at Pembroke Dock for at least eight years after the take-over, and possibly for some years later. Alfred Cozens continued as station master at Lamphey until June 1926; he was probably the last P&T man to retire. Another former company servant was B. Howells, a Whitland goods guard and checker. In a working day lasting from 5.30 am to 4.30 pm he made one journey from Whitland to Pembroke Dock and back, and spent a good deal of time checking and abstracting invoices. Apparently in his early days on the P&T the company deducted 1/- from his pay if he made any errors! Later the company decided to accept the burden of the mistake. In spite of such memories, even after retirement, Pembroke & Tenby men seem to have retained a keen interest in their line. As G.W.J. Potter has recorded, in 1914, when a Mr Fox was station master at Tenby, the P&T's second station master there, Mr Bowen, frequently appeared to witness the arrival of the London

express. At that date Mr Bowen was said to be "hale and hearty and
. . . a prominent man in the affairs of the town".

In south Pembrokeshire, as elsewhere, the onset of World War I
brought changes. At the end of the summer of 1914 the railmotor
services were withdrawn, and the halts at Lydstep and Beavers Hill
were closed with effect from 23rd September. Troop trains became an
even more frequent sight, several such special workings running to
Pembroke Dock in the first weeks of the war. Hostilities also caused
the daily Fishguard–Rosslare sailings to be suspended, with the
result that the morning boat train from Paddington to Fishguard was
diverted to terminate at Pembroke Dock. The arrangement was to last
for well over forty years, and in spite of slight alterations in the train's
Paddington departure time even after World War II the service was
still known to P&T line men as "The Boat"! Not surprisingly, summer
passenger services declined during wartime, but freight traffic ex-
panded considerably. Stores, materials and munitions required by
the Navy and Army kept the railway busy through the day and, for a
period, late at night. Track and signalling alterations were soon
needed, notably at Templeton and Pembroke. A few years before the
war a crossing loop and signal box had been installed at Templeton,
primarily to allow freight trains to pass, and to prevent the line being
obstructed by engines then being used for banking over Cold Blow
summit. In 1915 it was decided to extend the crossing loop, and to
provide a refuge siding and second platform. At Pembroke accommodation was improved in 1917 by the laying in of the sidings on the
down side east of the station. At the same time Pembroke's signal box
was replaced by a new timber-built box with a sixteen lever frame.

During the 1920s the railway soon recovered passenger traffic lost
during the war, but freight business gradually declined. By this
period the Black Rock quarries at Tenby were closed, and in 1924 the
silica firebrick works at Templeton also shut. This was a serious loss,
because for many years it provided thousands of bricks each week for
rail delivery all over the country. However, in 1926, the year of the
General Strike*, when there was no movement on most Pembrokeshire lines for several days, the greatest blow fell. This was the
sudden closure of the Royal Dockyard at Pembroke Dock; quite apart
from the damaging effect on railway business, the closure caused
immense hardship and distress to hundreds of local families. Just to
make matters worse, the coal industry was also in decline and,
whereas in 1920 about half the coal produced around Saundersfoot
was moved away by rail, the flow was much less by the end of the
decade. Indeed, after Bonvilles Court colliery closed on 17th April,
1930, coal traffic at Saundersfoot was negligible for several years until
two or three nearby pits were briefly reopened. The industry, and the

---

* A very few trains did run on the P&T line. According to the *Western Telegraph* of 20th
May, 1926 two Milford trawler men drove a train from Goodwick to Tenby on 10th
May, 1926.

Saundersfoot Railway, finally closed in 1939.

Fortunately tourist and military traffic made good the deterioration in freight, and by the late 1920s the public timetable hardly did justice to the volume of business. In June, 1928 the passenger timetable showed eight trains each way between Whitland and Pembroke Dock, no less than three of which conveyed through carriages between Paddington and Pembroke Dock. According to Bradshaw one train each way (9.20 am up from Pembroke Dock, and 3.14 pm down from Whitland) was designated the "Tenby and Carmarthen Bay Express". In addition there were three trains a day in each direction between Tenby and Pembroke Dock at least one of which was worked by an auto train. The auto train, which was one class only, also operated two of the services each way over the whole route on a weekday diagram which apparently began with the 9.15 am down from Whitland and finished with the 7.10 pm up from Pembroke Dock. The halts at Lydstep and Beavers Hill were mentioned in the timetable, public services having been restored from 9th July and 1st December, 1923 respectively, Sunday trains in June 1928, comprised three afternoon trains each way between Tenby and Pembroke Dock.

Such a crowded timetable told only a part of the story. During the 'twenties and 'thirties the traffic worked on summer weekends was fantastic. Special and relief workings vied with train loads of territorials, and even boy scouts, to make their way down the P&T. Most of the tourist traffic ended at Tenby or Saundersfoot; Penally, Manorbier and Pembroke were the usual destinations for the military. The arrival of the Swindon Works holiday trains was an annual event; the passengers travelled on free passes, and many spent their fortnight largely in the company of their workmates! The principal mail train might run with anything up to three reliefs all the way from Paddington. At Whitland these huge trains would sometimes extend back over the level crossing, and have to be divided again. The first part would then go through to Pembroke Dock, whilst the second ran only to Tenby, perhaps hauled by a prairie tank. Often troop trains ran in several parts also — for example the first with the men, the second with the baggage, and maybe a third with armoured vehicles loaded on flat wagons. At the height of the summer up trains frequently had to wait for down trains at Tenby: it was not unknown for a train to wait for two the other way to pass, and then encounter other down trains in passing loops at Saundersfoot and Narberth. At such time Whitland was a veritable hive of activity: so much train marshalling took place that a pilot locomotive might be required right round the clock! In the summers of the 1930s the junction was in its heyday: the station, the sheds and the yards dominated the life of the town, and railwaymen were the backbone of the local economy.

With such a volume of traffic through Whitland the locomotive shed inevitably grew in importance. The depot at Tenby declined, however, and was closed with effect from 12th September, 1932. Weight restrictions on the line were eased, and the P&T route was designated "red" on the Great Western colour code for axle loadings on their railways. The section between Saundersfoot and Tenby, being rather steep and sinuous, was designated "dotted red", and heavier locomotives were restricted to a mere 20 mph on that stretch.

Now motive power appeared of a size unimaginable in the days of the P&TR. Before World War I Dean 0–6–0s and 2–4–0s (including engines of the "806" and "Stella" classes) had been a common sight, and at least one train a day each way had been hauled by a 4–4–0 based at Neyland. After the war the 4–4–0s and 0–6–0s were still in evidence, but in the mid or late 1920s the much newer 43XX 2–6–0s and 45XX 2–6–2 tank locomotives took over many services — often hauling remarkable assortments of rolling stock, including modern and clerestory coaches, and even four-wheeled suburban stock. A little earlier the experimental 4–4–2T No. 4600 frequently travelled the line, actually being based at Pembroke Dock from January 1919, until June 1922.

By the 1930s larger prairie tanks had appeared, and in March, 1930, No. 5159 was allocated to Pembroke Dock. "Hall" class 4–6–0s also appeared, and even "Castles" made occasional visits. No. 5035 *Coity Castle* is believed to have been the first such visitor, working to Pembroke Dock at a time of motive power shortage. Although it coped with the clearances, the turntable at Pembroke Dock was a squeeze. Thereafter "Castle" excursions were rare, and usually resulted in the engine returning tender first. This was an uncommon sight at the time, because locomotives seldom ran round at Pembroke Dock. Usually they propelled stock back from the down platform until free to run on to the turntable road, ready for turning. The guard then allowed the coaches to run back into the station.

Operating the P&T line had its lighter moments. On one occasion the Pembroke signalman gave a goods train right of way out of Pembroke ahead of the up Mail. As it left, the guard, who was the worse for drink, slipped between the brakevan and the platform, and was lucky to escape serious injury. Meanwhile the train went on through Manorbier and was stopped at Tenby. In order not to impede the Mail the driver took on a porter as guard and ran the train hard to Whitland, eventually entering the bay platform there. The up Mail followed close behind into the main platform — carrying the guard. He carried tattered garments in one hand, and his lamp and flags in the other!

Banking out of Whitland provided the fireman of the pilot engine with a fine opportunity for mischief at the expense of the train engine crew. A strong smell in the confines of Narberth tunnel could encourage them to work much harder; urine on a heated shovel was said to produce the desired effect! The railwayman often had girlfriends in the district, and sometimes one would become pregnant. On one occasion a solicitor appeared on Narberth platform to serve a paternity order. He was spotted by the offending fireman, who hung out of the locomotive on the opposite side. The lawyer guessed what was going on, and waited for him to return with the down train from Whitland. Another incident, with potentially serious consequences, was reported by the *Haverfordwest & Milford Haven Telegraph* in April 1939. A railway van ran away during shunting at Pembroke Dock and fell into 30 feet of water — presumably at Hobbs Point, because the splash was seen from the opposite shore. As the van was said to be loaded with ten tons of cement it must have posed a nice problem for recovery!

In his book *Behind the Steam* Driver Bill Morgan described how a fireman was suspended for six days for forgetting to pick up the single line staff at Whitland. In fact Whitland West had the only picking up post for the electric staff; the P&T route was otherwise a "give and take road", the staffs being exchanged by hand. Staff instruments were located in signal boxes except at Manorbier, Saundersfoot and Templeton, where they were placed in station offices. Later electric token apparatus replaced the staff equipment on sections between Pembroke and Saundersfoot. By now the only movable distant signals were those protecting the crossings at Beavers Hill and Manorbier Newton, and all the P&TR's Mackenzie & Holland signalling had disappeared. The track was now maintained by gangs based at Pembroke, Tenby and Narberth using motor trolleys.

The timetable for July 1938, shows that tourist traffic continued to grow. On Saturdays there were ten down trains and nine up trains over the full length of the line, of which two ran to or from Paddington and one to or from Birmingham. In addition there was one train each way between Tenby and Pembroke Dock. Weekday services consisted of six trains in each direction over the whole route, two conveying through carriages to or from Paddington. There was also one train from Whitland to Tenby and back, two from Tenby to Pembroke Dock and back, and a third each way over the latter section on Wednesdays only. The Sunday service consisted of two return trips between Pembroke Dock and Tenby only, and one each way over the whole line, although there was another on the last two Sundays of July which conveyed through carriages from Birmingham in the down direction and through carriages to Birmingham and

Paddington in the up direction.

By the late 1930s plans were afoot for a new station and locomotive shed at Whitland. The outbreak of World War II put an end to the plans for the station, and stopped the scheme for the new shed after only a turntable and a few sidings had been laid in the fork between Fishguard and the Pembroke Dock lines. Instead the existing engine shed was repaired, the rounded roof being replaced by a pitched corrugated metal roof. A timber canopy continued to suffice for the coaling plant. Wartime measures included some other economies: Golden Hill Platform closed with effect from 5th February, 1940. At about the same date the Bonville's Court colliery siding was formally closed, but as it had seen modest traffic for several years the closure was not a great loss.

In World War II Pembroke Dock became an important oil storage depot, and the garrison was enlarged. This was hardly a blessing, because the town attracted air raids. There are still bitter memories of the bombing, especially between July 1940 and June 1941. Although the main targets were oil tanks, casualties in the town were considerable, and the station master's house was one of many to be seriously damaged. The railway kept working, and was busy with extra freight, stores and armoured vehicles, not to mention the numerous troop trains. To accommodate military traffic a new loop and ground frame was brought into use at Pembroke on 25th June, 1941, a ground frame and extended siding space at Pembroke Dock was operational from 22nd July, 1942.

Troop trains on the P & T were notoriously slow, sometimes making way for freight as well as ordinary passenger services. 43XX 2-6-0s, or "2251" or Dean Goods 0-6-0s were often turned out for such workings, but it is said that late in the war a Stanier 2-8-0 was involved in an unpublicised troop train accident at Narberth. Large and small prairie tank engines continued to work on the new reduced public passenger service, and the 45XX class also worked on the Dockyard Extension. In contrast to 1938, the timetable for January 1944 showed no Saturday services at all, and weekday trains comprised five each way over the full length of the line. Two of these conveyed Paddington through coaches. On Sundays there was just one train down from Whitland at 6.35 am, and one train up from Pembroke Dock at 6.00 pm. Perhaps surprisingly, the halts at Lydstep and Beavers Hill were advertised.

Once the war was over passenger traffic began to revive, and freight traffic again went into decline. The severe winter of 1947 caused some disruption in west Wales as elsewhere, but the P & T line suffered less than many others. The politicians were active, however, and hardly had the railway got back into its stride under private enterprise than Parliament approved nationalisation of the railways. On 1st January, 1948 British Railways was born and the Great Western was no more.

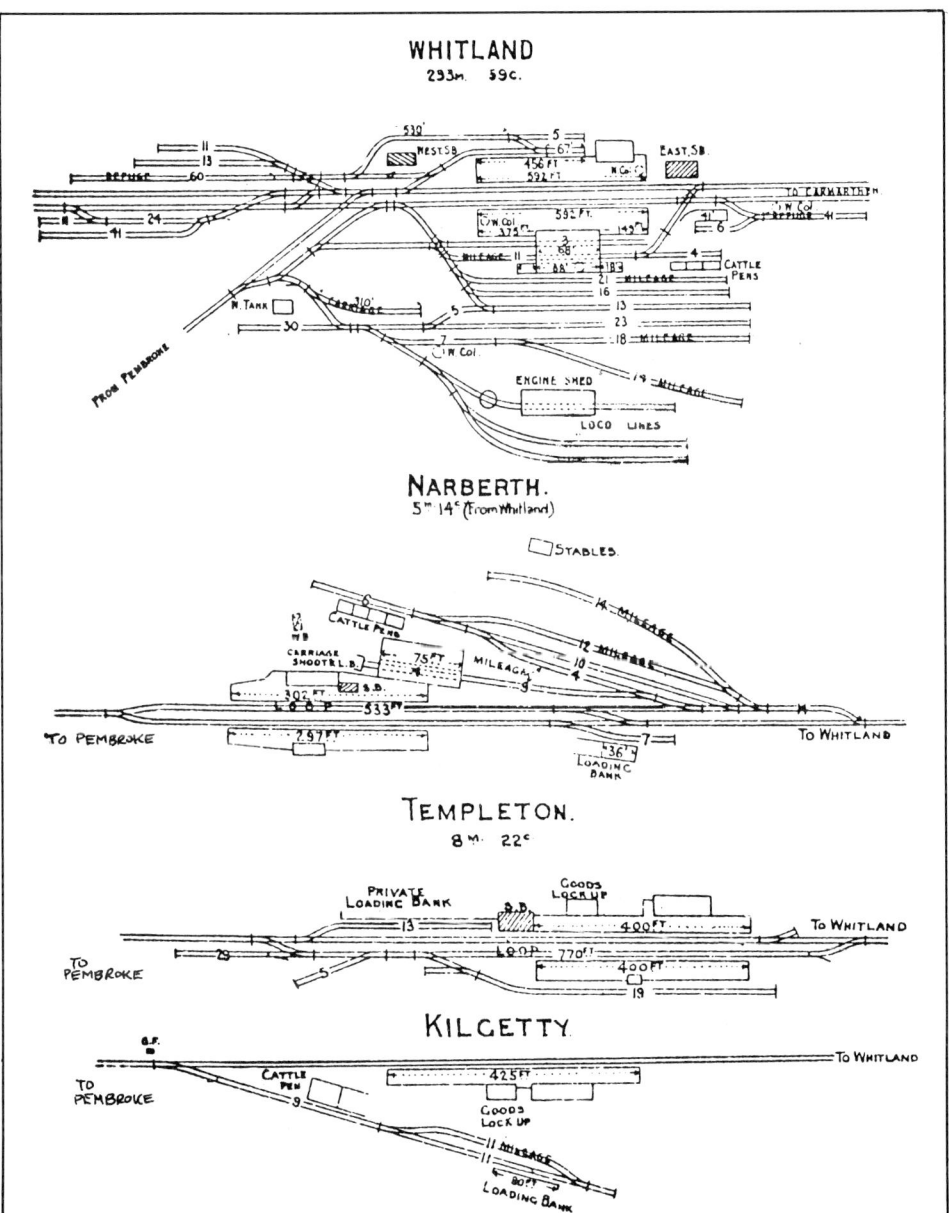

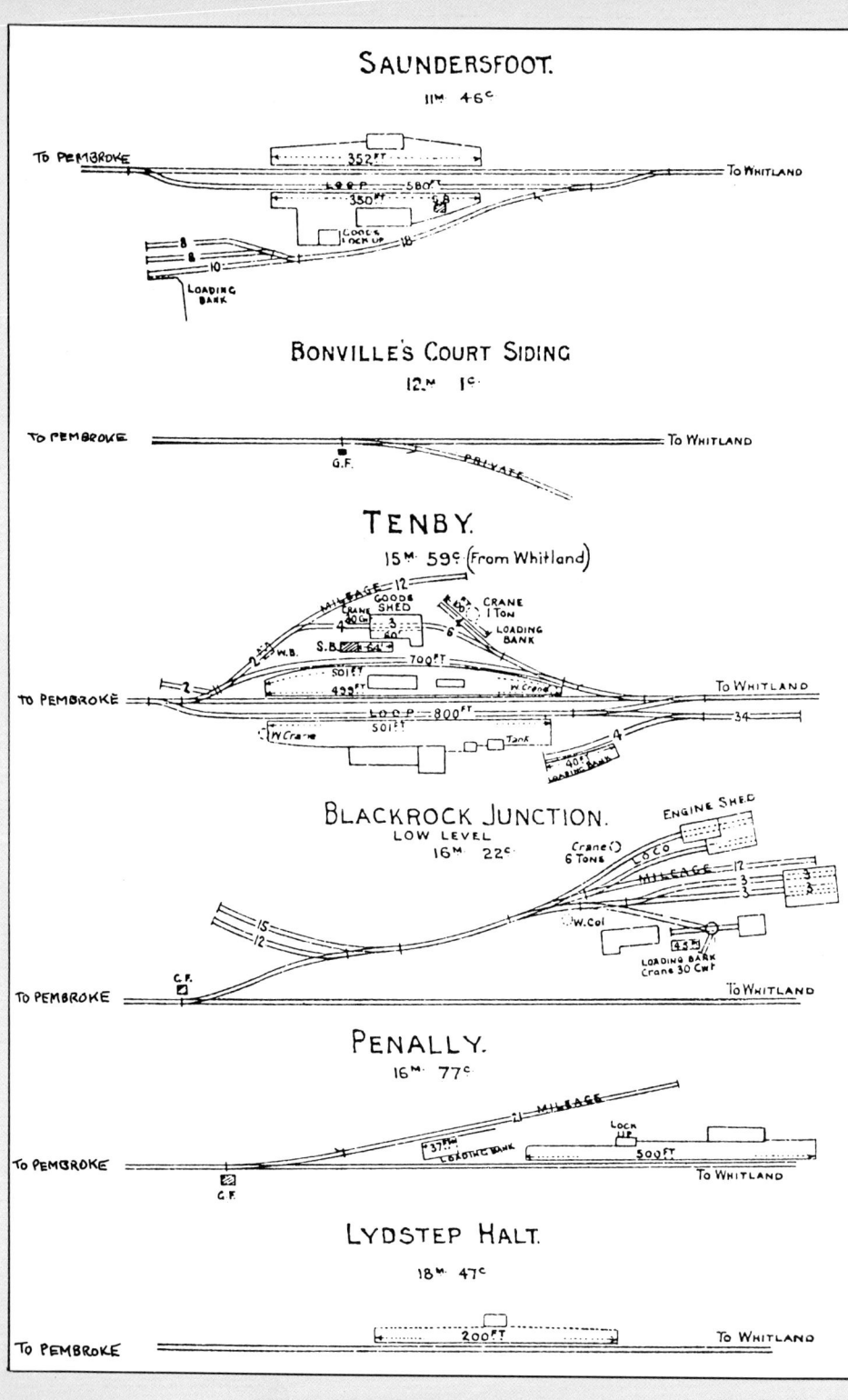

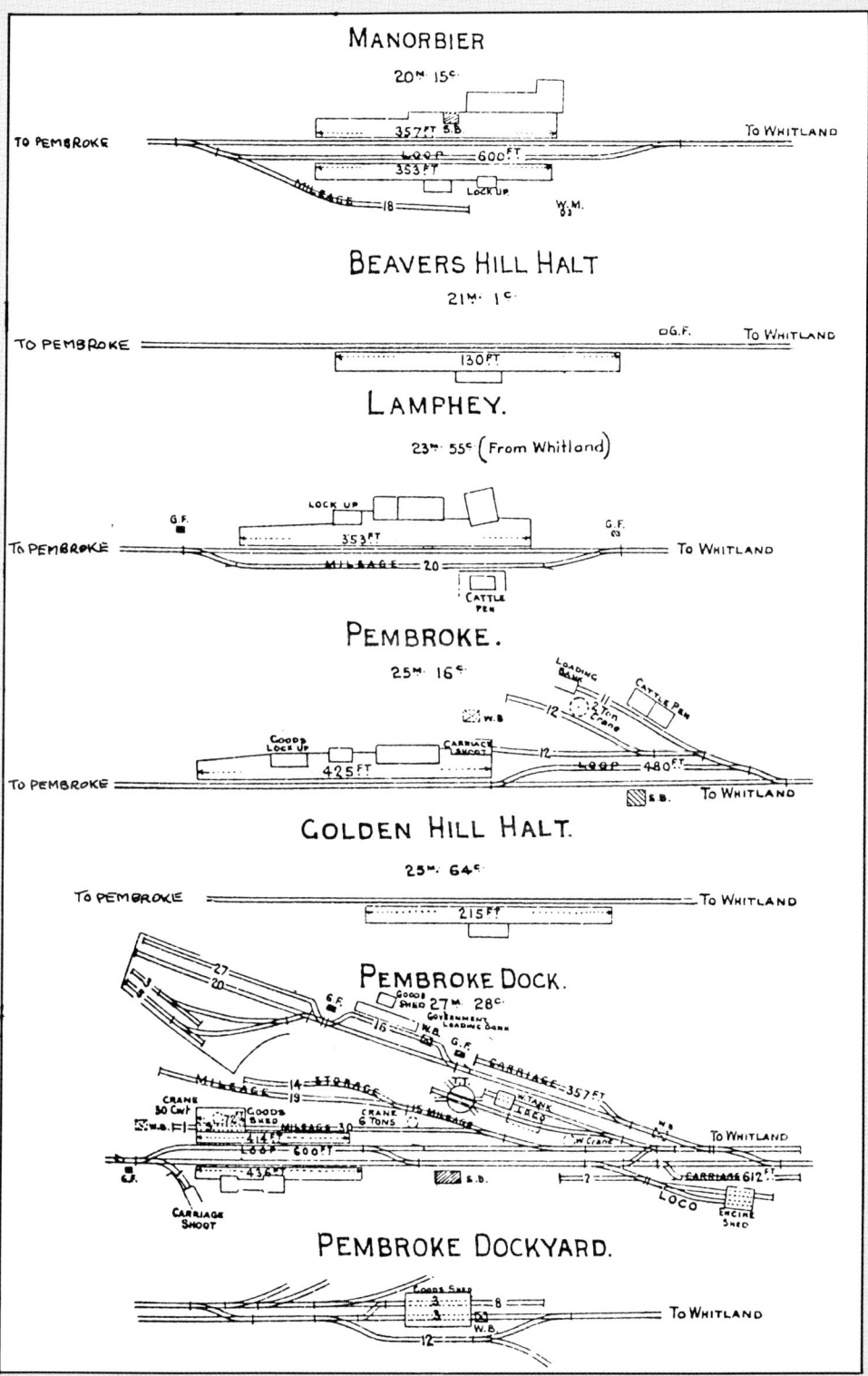

Chapter Twelve
British Railways' Pembroke Dock Branch

Nationalisation brought no immediate changes to the Pembroke & Tenby line, although the post-war revival in tourism brought back summer Saturday through trains, running from places like Shrewsbury, Birmingham and Paddington. By the early 1950s the line had recovered something of the atmosphere of the 1930s, and in 1953 came the introduction of the "Pembroke Coast Express". This train of modern stock, sporting the chocolate and cream colours of the Great Western, was worked to and from Pembroke Dock by a tender locomotive embellished with a decorative headboard. Once established "the Coast", as it was sometimes called, left Paddington daily on the down journey at 10.55 am arriving at Pembroke Dock at 5.26 pm. The up train left Pembroke Dock at 1.05 pm and, after calling at all stations to Whitland except Beavers Hill, reached Paddington at 7.45 pm. Overnight the coaches were stabled at Pembroke Dock, whilst the locomotive (at first a 43XX 2–6–0 but later sometimes a "Manor" 4–6–0) usually returned to Whitland shed.

Although the introduction of the "Pembroke Coast Express" was encouraging, by 1955 there was mention of economies. In April that year Penally station became partially unstaffed, and two months later Kilgetty was accorded the same treatment. On 2nd January, 1956 the halt at Lydstep was officially closed, and a week later Lamphey became partially unstaffed. In contrast to these cuts, plans were afoot for the reconstruction of the stations at Whitland and Tenby; the rebuilding of Whitland had been mooted for years, and was long overdue. The first step, however, was the provision of a modern signal box at Tenby, and this was opened on 23rd May, 1956. The rest of the work at Tenby was not put in hand until 1959, and it included the replacement of buildings on the up platform with a prefabricated timber building very similar in style to those recently erected at Whitland. In addition the existing structure on the down platform at Tenby was given an enlarged porch and a renovated ticket hall, which was partitioned from the waiting room by a glass screen. The reconstruction, which included a new concrete footbridge and fluorescent lighting, was finished in 1960.

The next decade was one of considerable change. Although diesels were sometimes seen on summer Saturdays in 1959 and subsequent years, in the autumn of 1963 a regular diesel multiple unit service began to operate between Whitland and Pembroke Dock. Steam survived as the dominant form of traction just long enough to witness the P&T's centenary, but the closure of the shed at Pembroke Dock in September 1963 marked the end of regular steam working over the line. The last steam locomotive pulled away from Pembroke Dock at

5.55 pm on Sunday, 8th September, but few people were present to witness the departure of 61XX 2–6–2T No. 6118. From the next day diesels reigned supreme. Whitland shed retained a diesel pilot engine for local shunting until closure in January 1966. Thereafter Whitland enginemen had to sign on at Carmarthen, even though many of their turns were to take them onto the Pembroke & Tenby! By then the GWR's six road shed at Carmarthen had been closed following the demise of the steam hauled service over the M&M route from Aberystwyth in December 1964.

The Beeching era on British Railways was now at its height, and as these changes were taking place further economies were put into effect. Goods business at Templeton, Saundersfoot, Penally and Lamphey came to an end on 2nd December, 1963, and Templeton, Penally and Beavers Hill were closed completely on 15th June, 1964. Soon after on 28th September the same year, the stations at Narberth, Kilgetty, Saundersfoot, Manorbier and Lamphey became unstaffed. As a result of these changes camping coaches were withdrawn from Saundersfoot, Penally and Manorbier. Manorbier was closed for freight on 30th November, 1964, and on 7th June, 1965, goods traffic at Narberth, Kilgetty and Tenby Lower Yard also came to an end. For the final months business at these three places consisted almost entirely of coal, although it is believed that Tenby Lower Yard was sometimes used for rolling stock later in the summer of 1965. Freight traffic at Tenby station lasted only a little longer, being withdrawn on 7th November, 1966. By this time the freight service consisted of no more than one train each way on weekdays only.

On 3rd October, 1965, the loops and signal boxes at Narberth, Templeton, Saundersfoot and Manorbier were abolished. Thereafter the railway was operated with sections from Whitland to Tenby, and Tenby to Pembroke. Most of the redundant track was lifted in 1966, and the turntable and carriage sidings at Whitland were also removed. By now there was no longer a need for both platforms at Pembroke Dock, and on 24th August, 1966, the signal box was closed, and replaced by a ground frame and "one train" working (from Pembroke) introduced. The north (or up) platform line was reduced to a siding, and the south platform line maintained for all passenger services. The new ground frame, and the ground frame at Llanion, provided access to the sidings, including the already rusty tracks leading to Hobbs Point and the Dockyard. In spite of disuse, these short branches were not closed officially until 1st January, 1969. The Hobbs Point line was then lifted entirely. The Dockyard Extension was allowed to remain in situ, apart from the removal of a length of track near Pembroke Dock station to enable stop blocks to be set up at the end of both platform roads.

In the summer of 1970 there was a welcome reversal of one decision in this depressing sequence of events. Penally reappeared in the passenger timetable with effect from 24th June, 1970. In that year and the following year trains called only between June and September, but in 1972 it was decided to leave the station open throughout the year. By now Penally's station building had been converted into a private dwelling and fenced off from the platform, so that the main expense in reopening was the provision of a wooden shelter for waiting passengers. At about the same period pink and grey concrete waiting shelters replaced earlier buildings at Kilgetty, Saundersfoot, Lamphey and Pembroke. Pembroke's rather fine station building had been destroyed by fire shortly before, at a time when the station was otherwise enjoying a spell of prosperity. The construction of the large oil-fired Pembroke power station created, for a while, regular traffic in cement. A large cement silo was erected in the up side goods yard, and the sidings were crowded with cement wagons. As soon as construction finished, though, the traffic ceased, and Pembroke's passing loop and down side goods sidings were removed. On 5th September, 1971, as part of the economies, the signal box was closed, "no signalman token" working being introduced, controlled from Tenby. This was extended through to Pembroke Dock, replacing the former "one train" working between Pembroke and Pembroke Dock.

In spite of these cuts, the outlook for the railway was becoming brighter. Whereas in the 1960s the complete closure of the P&T line, at least between Tenby and Pembroke Dock, appeared to be a real possibility, by the early 1970s there were signs that the railway had a future. Sunday services were re-introduced, and special excursion traffic also increased. At Whitland a long delayed re-signalling scheme was put into effect, and the track layout improved to enable up trains from Pembroke Dock to use the down bay platform rather than cross to the up main. Colour light signals were provided on the main line and on 2nd September, 1972, a modern signal box formerly located at Danygraig was brought into use on a site opposite the old East box. Complete colour light signalling between Whitland and Carmarthen was established later in the summer of 1978, at which time automatic lifting barriers were installed at St Clears and Sarnau, and the adjacent signal boxes were abolished.

In 1973, in an effort to encourage more holidaymakers, British Rail decided to make Tenby a "Golden Rail resort". Bookings flourished, and two years later a summer Saturdays through service between York and Tenby was introduced. This began on 14th June, 1975, with some remarkable ceremonial at Tenby. The crowded station was decorated with bunting, a brass band played, and the Mayors of both towns were in attendance to welcome the new service. After that, it settled down to regular operation, the up service leaving Tenby at 9.10 am, and the down service reaching Tenby at 4.10 pm. The train normally consisted of Mark II rolling stock and even as late as 1975 was sometimes hauled by a "Western" class diesel. With the withdrawal of the diesel hydraulics, the Brush-built class 47 diesels became the customary motive power for this train, and for the occasional military special which still appeared on the line.

By the mid 1970s the freight service was very sparse, being reduced to two trains a week, on Mondays and Thursdays. In the summer of 1977 these trains, usually hauled by class 37 diesels, were scheduled to leave Whitland at 8.45 am and reach Pembroke Dock at 10.10 am, after short stops at Tenby and Manorbier. The up service was timed to leave Pembroke Dock at 12.25 pm, running to Pembroke to shunt between 12.35 and 1.20. After brief stops at Manorbier and Tenby the train ran through to Whitland by 2.40 and Carmarthen Junction by 3.20. The timetable was similar in 1978, but that summer it was announced that the service would end with effect from 31st October, 1978, freight facilities being withdrawn from Pembroke Dock and Pembroke. In fact the service was not withdrawn until 31st December, 1978. Thereafter freight wagons appeared on the line only on engineer's trains, or on special services for the military.

In November 1977, the British & Irish Steam Packet Co. of Dublin came out with the surprise announcement of a £4 million plan to develop part of the old Pembroke dockyard as a ferry terminal. This scheme, which gave Pembroke Dock its most encouraging news for a generation, anticipated the transfer of the Swansea–Cork ferry service to Pembroke Dock by May 1979, with the provision of good rail connections. The shipping company and the local authority naturally wanted to make use of the branch to Pembroke Dock, and some even advocated the re-opening of the Dockyard Extension to give direct access to the new ferry terminal. British Rail, on the other hand, claimed that this would require costly improvements to the branch, and instead suggested the provision of a fast bus service from Haverfordwest to Pembroke Dock via the recently completed Cleddau road bridge. Coming so soon after the withdrawal of the freight service, this proposal was viewed with some suspicion, and many wondered if BR's real intention was to close the Tenby–Pembroke Dock section. After some months of uncertainty it was agreed that the somewhat decayed station at Pembroke Dock should be renovated, but that work on the old Dockyard Extension was not justified, as buses would suffice to move passengers to and from the ferry.

The ferry service between Pembroke Dock and Cork began on 22nd May, 1979, using the new B&I flagship, the *Connacht*. Maybe a few passengers appreciated the ironies of history as the vessel docked within sight of the long abandoned terminal at Neyland. In fact the new ferry terminal was not completed fully until late 1979, and the much delayed renovation of Pembroke Dock station was not finished until the next year. Refurbished at a cost of £110,000 and including a new booking office, it was formally opened by Cllr Tom George, Chairman of Dyfed County Council, in May 1980. In the same month B&I line inaugurated a ferry service between Pembroke Dock and Rosslare.

With all the advantages of hindsight,May 1980 may be regarded as the zenith of the new ferry services. From B&I's viewpoint they were never an outstanding success. Even before the end of 1980 changes of vessel, poor timekeeping and union troubles gave the Rosslare service a reputation for unreliability, and the following year both routes were beset by problems. In January, 1982, after heavy losses, B&I line announced that the *Innisfallen* would operate reduced services from Pembroke Dock to both Cork and Rosslare. Unfortunately the *Innisfallen* was not equal to the task and after more difficulties the Cork service was withdrawn in 1983 and not reinstated in 1984. Meanwhile competition between B&I Line at Pembroke Dock and Sealink at Fishguard was not proving beneficial to either party, with the result that an agreement was reached in February, 1985, to rationalize their sailings. These arrangements left Pembroke Dock without sailings for six weeks of the year, an ominous state of affairs confirmed later in the year by an announcement that the two companies would soon share facilities at Fishguard. Protests and representations from South Pembrokeshire were of no avail, and the last sailings from Pembroke Dock to Rosslare were made in January, 1986. Since then there has been talk of a new ferry service between Pembroke Dock and Spain, but at the time of writing there is no sign of this becoming a reality.

The sorry saga of the Pembroke Dock ferry services was reflected in disappointment on British Rail. In the early days an enhanced train service proved to be over optimistic, and one train — the 1.25 am Pembroke Dock–Whitland — was quietly withdrawn after running on a number of nights without any passengers at all. Indeed, it is doubtful if the ferry services ever generated any very significant traffic for the Pembroke & Tenby line. Nevertheless there was one bright moment in the midst of it all. In the summer of 1983 an early morning service was provided from Pembroke using a "125" High Speed Train. This train preceded the early passenger service to Pembroke Dock, and was placed in a siding at the terminus to allow for the passage of the ordinary service train. As soon as this train had returned to Tenby (7.00 am from Pembroke Dock), the points were released and the HST was allowed to start away to Pembroke to pick up its first fare paying passengers.

Sadly this glimpse of modernisation was not permitted to continue in 1984. The most modern coaching stock seen that year was a brand new railway carriage, said to be 95 ft long, conveyed on a low loader lorry destined for Dublin by the B&I ferry. The lorry attempted to enter the dockyard at the site of the former Dockyard Extension Railway but, after much manoeuvring, it was eventually taken into the ferry terminal by the main entrance. For older inhabitants this occasion was a reminder of an earlier incident on the Dockyard Extension, in April 1956, when three passenger coaches ran away from Pembroke Dock station and derailed at the Water Street crossing. The leading coach struck a dentist's surgery, but the residents (and the occupant of the dentist's chair) were unhurt.

In July, 1985, Tenby station played host to British Rail's special exhibition train celebrating the 150th anniversary of the Great Western Railway. Although the display was appropriate, and appreciated, it must be wondered if the P&TR itself will ever be honoured by a full scale exhibition in the district. Notwithstanding a small but interesting display in Tenby Museum, the enterprise of Davies & Roberts, the commitment of the Barrow family, and the faithful service of men like Isaac Smedley merit more recognition in the area served by the railway. Meanwhile it is hard to speculate about the long term future of the line. The original section west of Tenby has looked vulnerable for some time, having the disadvantages of the tunnel at Pembroke, the level crossing at Manorbier, and an awkward bridge over the A4139 at Lydstep. Against this, it must be noted that the section still occasionally carries military traffic, and in September, 1986, there was also talk of the possibility of redeveloping a freight terminal in the goods yard at Pembroke Dock. Less hopefully, it was reported in the same month that Tenby was to lose its status as a "Golden Rail" resort, as a result both of changes in holiday patterns, and of a lack of suitable hotel accommodation throughout the year. In the meantime British Rail staff are doing their best to maintain business, and in both 1984 and 1985 Tenby station was a prizewinner in the annual best kept station and customer care competition. With such encouragement from railway staff, it is very much to be hoped that more people will use the route throughout the year to the benefit of the local community, as well as the Pembroke & Tenby line.

Pembroke & Tenby Railway.

Statement showing the Train Mileage, Revenue, also Locomotive & Carriage Department Expenditure during the following half years:—

(Swindon 6.7.96)

Half year ended	Train Miles run			Revenue — Traffic Receipts				Expenses	Carriage & Wagon Department		
	With Passengers	With Goods &c	Total	Passengers £ (Average per Train Mile s.d.)	Goods £ (s.d.)	Sundries £ (s.d.)	Total £ (s.d.)	Locomotive Department £ (per train mile d.)	Carriage £ (d.)	Wagon £ (d.)	Total £ (d.)
1892											
June 30	41746	24468	66214	6543 3/1·0	5304 4/1·1	273	12120 3/4·9	2084 7·35	263 1·31	257 2·05	520 1·11
December 31	47901	25141	73042	9583 4/0·4	5221 4/1·0	315 1·0	15119 4/2·0	2488 8·17	185 ·83	348 2·60	543 1·41
1893											
June 30	41345	24322	65667	7110 3/5·2	5237 4/3·7	278 1·0	12625 3/10·1	2282 1·34	301 1·41	294 2·19	595 2·14
December 31	50944	25805	76749	9141 3/7·0	5551 4/3·0	323 1·0	15018 3/11·0	2285 7·14	216 1·14	368 3·41	584 1·82
1894											
June 30	45609	29391	75000	6815 3/-	5736 3/10·1	264	12815 3/5·0	2475 7·92	453 2·34	457 3·43	910 2·91
December 31	49739	26619	76358	9341 3/9·0	5484 4/1·2	316	15141 3/11·6	2396 7·53	220 1·06	457 4·12	677 2·12
1895											
June 30	48110	26152	74262	6970 2/10·4	5150 3/11·2	281	12401 3/4·0	2457 7·94	331 1·65	325 2·91	656 2·12
December 31	51622	28473	80095	10010 3/10·5	6312 4/5·2	542 1·0	16864 4/2·5	2924 6·94	213 ·99	453 3·41	666 1·99

Statement of Train Mileage, Revenue and Expenditure, dated 1896.

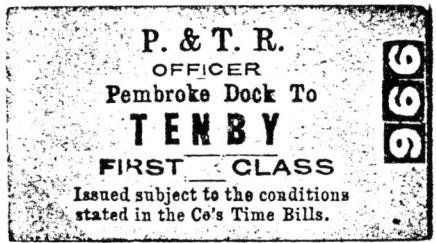

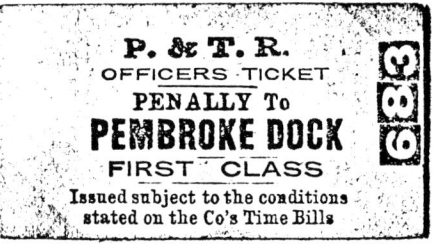

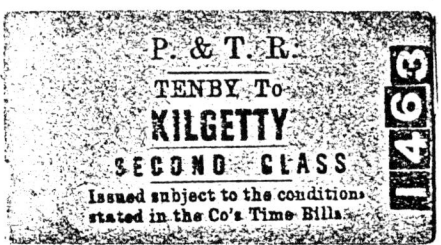

Selection of Tickets.

Appendix One: Working Timetables

Working Timetable of May 1913

PEMBROKE DOCK. — Week Days

	6 London Excursion. W		7 Empty Cattle Wgr.		8		9 London Excursion. W		10 Passenger.		11
STATIONS.	arr.	dep.	arr.	dep.			arr.	dep.	arr.	dep.	dep.
Whitland	A.M.	9 10	A.M. 9 55	A.M. 9 55			A.M. 10 35	A.M. 10 40	A.M. 10 50	A.M. 10 50	
Narberth		9 21	9 57	10 5			10 57	10 57	11 1	11	
Stop Board					Narberth Fair Days only.						
Templeton							10 57	10 57	11 5	11	
Kilgetty		9 42					10 2	11 10	11 10	11 14	
Saundersfoot											
Boavile's Court Siding											
Stop Board											
Tenby	9 52	9 55					10 28	11 21	11 21	11 28	11 32
Black Rock Siding											
Penally		10						11 30	11 30	11 41	
Lydstep Halt											
Manorbier		10 7						11 38	11 38	11 47	
Beavers Hill Halt											
Lamphey											
Pembroke Loop											
Pembroke							11 5	11 54	11 54	11 59	
Golden Hill Platform											
Pembroke Dock	10 15						11 10	12 0	12 0		

W — SUSPENDED. Y — Runs last Monday in each month.

TO WHITLAND. — Week Days

	7		8 Passenger.		9		10		11 Passenger.		12 Workmen's Train SO
STATIONS.	arr.	dep.	arr.	dep.					arr.	dep.	dep.
Pembroke Dock			A.M.	A.M. 10 20					P.M.	P.M. 12 15	P.M. 12 35
Golden Hill Platform			10 27	10 30					12 22	12 24	12 42
Pembroke				10 33						12	12 45
Pembroke Loop											
Lamphey			10 43	10 42					12 34	12 36	
Beavers Hill Halt											
Manorbier			10 45	10 50					12 42	12 41	
Lydstep Halt											
Penally											
Tenby			10 53	10 58					12 47	12 55	1 10
Boarville's Court Siding											
Saundersfoot											
Kilgetty			11 8	11 12					1 9		
Templeton										1 20	
Stop Board											
Narberth			11 31	11 34					1 36		
Whitland			11 43						1 50		

WHITLAND TO — Down Trains.

Distance from Whitland		STATIONS.	Station No.	1 Workman. B	2 Passenger.		3 Passenger.		4 Goods.		5 C 7.0 a.m. Carmarthen Cattle Empties Y
M.	C.			dep.	arr.	dep.	arr.	dep.	arr.	dep.	dep.
		Whitland	3699	A.M.	A.M. 5 55	A.M. 6			A.M. 7 15	A.M. 7 0	A.M. 7 40
5	6	Narberth	3756		6	6			7 30	7 30	7 20
6	9	Stop Board	3760		6 15	6 15			7 48	7 50	8 25
8	57	Templeton	3761		6 22	6 22			8 2	8 10	8
12	46	Kilgetty	3762		6 27	6 27			8 13	8 22	P
		Saundersfoot	3763								
		Boarville's Court Siding	3764		6 24				8 40		
16	59	Tenby	3765		6 36	6 41		9 12	C R		P
17	32	Black Rock Siding	3766								
18	25	Penally	3767		6 45	6 45		9 16			
19	47	Lydstep Halt	3768								
20	51	Manorbier	3769		6 53	6 53		9 24	10 20	10 11	P
21	10	Beavers Hill Halt	3770								
23	55	Lamphey	3771		7	7		9 33		10 11	
		Pembroke Loop	3772	6 22							
25	14	Pembroke	3773	6 24	7 3	7 5		9 38	11 10	11 25	P
26		Golden Hill Platform	3773	6 27				9 41			
27	25	Pembroke Dock	3770	6 31	7 10	7 10		9 45	11 32		

J ST. 5774, 575, 594, 628. Y Runs last Monday in each month.

PEMBROKE DOCK — Up Trains.

	STATIONS.	1 Empty Train.		2 Cattle and Goods.		3		4		5 Passenger.	
		arr.	dep.	arr.	dep.					arr.	dep.
	Pembroke Dock	A.M.	A.M. 6 10	A.M. 6 55	A.M. 7 20					A.M.	A.M. 7 45
	Golden Hill Platform										7 48
	Pembroke	6 15	6 22	7 2	7 20					7 54	7 54
	Pembroke Loop										
	Lamphey			C R						8	8
	Manorbier									8 6	8 10
	Lydstep Halt										
	Penally			C R							
	Tenby			7 50	8 51					8 15	8 16
	Black Rock Siding			9 1	9 10						
	Boarville's Court Siding			9 2	9 20					8 27	
	Saundersfoot									8 32	
	Kilgetty			9 30	9 55					8 35	
	Templeton										8 45
	Stop Board			10 10	10 31						
	Narberth			10 31	10 31					8 58	
	Whitland			11 5							

WHITLAND TO PEMBROKE DOCK.

DOWN TRAINS.

STATIONS.

Whitland
Narberth
Stop Board
Templeton
Kilgety
Saundersfoot
Bourville's Court Siding
Stop Board
Penally
Black Rock Siding
Penally Halt
Lydstep Halt
Manorbier
Beavers Hill Halt
Lamphey
Pembroke Loop
Pembroke
Golden Hill Platform
Pembroke Dock

Text on right margin: U Worked by Whitland Engine and Guard
P Commencing on June 1st

PEMBROKE DOCK TO WHITLAND.

UP TRAINS.

STATIONS.

Pembroke Dock
Golden Hill Platform
Pembroke
Pembroke Loop
Lamphey
Beavers Hill Halt
Manorbier
Lydstep Halt
Penally Halt
Black Rock Siding
Tenby
Bourville's Court Siding
Saundersfoot
Kilgety
Templeton
Stop Board
Narberth
Whitland

TENBY BRANCH.

FOR TIMES OF TRAINS SEE PAGES 110 TO 114.   Single Line worked by Electric Train Staff.

FOR PERMANENT SPEED RESTRICTIONS SEE PAGE 124.

Sections.	Crossing Stations.	Sections.	Crossing Stations.
Whitland and Narberth Narberth and Templeton Templeton and Saundersfoot Saundersfoot and Tenby	Whitland Narberth *Templeton Saundersfoot	Tenby and Manorbier Manorbier and Pembroke Pembroke and Pembroke Dock	Tenby Manorbier Pembroke and Pembroke Dock

* Two Passenger Trains must not cross at Templeton, but a Passenger Train and a Goods Train may do so; the Goods Train must be admitted into the Loop so that the Passenger Train can run over the Main Line.

Assistant Engines on Tenby Branch Trains.

Engines assisting Down Passenger or Goods Trains are to be taken off at Templeton, where the Trains are to stop specially for the purpose. Engines assisting Up Branch Passenger or Goods Trains are to be taken off at Narberth.

NORTH PEMBROKESHIRE BRANCHES.

FOR TIMES OF TRAINS SEE PAGES 118 TO 121.   FOR PERMANENT SPEED RESTRICTIONS SEE PAGE 123.

SINGLE LINE CLYNDERWEN TO LETTERSTON JUNCTION AND MANOROWEN TO FISHGUARD AND GOODWICK—Worked by Train Staff and Ticket and Block Telegraph, and Electric Train Staff as under :—

Spagnoletti System Clynderwen and Llanycefn, Tyer's Needle System Llanycefn and Rosebush, and Electric Staff System Rosebush and Letterston Jct. and Manorowen and Fishguard and Goodwick.

Form of Staff and Ticket.	Colour of Staff and Ticket.	SECTIONS.	Crossing Stations.
Hexagonal Triangular Electric Electric Electric	Green Blue	Clynderwen and Maenclochog Maenclochog and Rosebush Rosebush and Letterston. Letterston and Letterston Junction Manorowen and Fishguard & Goodwick	Clynderwen Maenclochog *Rosebush Letterston Fishguard and Goodwick

* Two Passenger Trains must not Cross at Rosebush, but a Passenger Train and a Goods Train may do so; the Goods Train must be admitted into the Loop so that the Passenger Train can run over the Main Line.

Llanycefn is an intermediate Block Telegraph Station.

All Up Trains (except Passenger) must stop at the bottom of the 1 in 27 gradient near the 4½ mile post.

CLARBESTON JUNCTION TO LETTERSTON JUNCTION.—Double Line Clarbeston Junction to Manorowen and Fishguard & Goodwick to Fishguard Harbour.

PEMBROKE DOCK. Week Days.

STATIONS.	18 Goods. RR		19	20 Workmen's Train. S		21	22 Workmen's Train. S		23 Mail Passenger.		24
	arr.	dep.		arr.	dep.		arr.	dep.	arr.	dep.	
	P.M.	P.M. 5 51			P.M.			P.M.	P.M.	P.M.		
Whitland	51.25	4 57							5 55	5 26		
Narberth										5 57		
Stop Board												
Templeton										5 46		
Kilgetty									5 55	5 55	6 33	
Saunderfoot										6 6 10		
Bourrile's Court Siding												
Stop Board												
Tenby										6 14		
Black Rock Siding												
Penally										6 21 6 24		
Lydstep Halt												
Beavers Hill Halt										6 31		
Lamphey												
Pembroke Loop												
Pembroke							5 31	5 10	6 34	6 38		
Golden Hill Platform							5 4	5 4		6 41		
Pembroke Dock							5 46			6 45		

TO WHITLAND. Week Days.

STATIONS.	19 Passenger.		20 Goods. RR		21	22 Workmen's Train. S		23 Mail Passenger.		24
	arr.	dep.	arr.	dep.		arr.	dep.	arr.	dep.	
	P.M.	P.M.	P.M.	P.M.		P.M.	P.M.	P.M.		
Pembroke Dock		3 40					5 32		6 0	
Golden Hill Platform	3 44	3 45					5 40	6 5	6 7	
Pembroke	3 47	3 49				5 21			6 11	
Pembroke Loop		3 54								
Lamphey		X 4 2						6 18	6 22	
Beavers Hill Halt										
Lydstep Halt									6 29	
Penally	4 8	4 10						6 32 6 36		
Black Rock Siding										
Tenby	4 13 4 15								6 41	
Bourrile's Court Siding										
Saunderfoot	4 28	4 31						6 53		
Kilgetty		4 34						6 55		
Templeton										
Stop Board			3 42						7 6	
Narberth	4 49	4 53	4 42	4 30					7 7	
Whitland				4 43				7 17		

WHITLAND TO — Down Trains.

STATIONS.	12 Goods. RR		13 Bristol Passenger.		14	15	16 Passenger.		17 Goods.	
	arr.	dep.	arr.	dep.			arr.	dep.	arr.	dep.
	P.M.	P.M.	A.M.	A.M.			P.M.	P.M.	P.M.	P.M. J
Whitland	12 25	12 55	10 19	12 17				2 11	1 25	1 10
Narberth							2 15	2 21	1 53	1 33
Stop Board								2 33		C R
Templeton			12 32	12 34			2 35	2 57	R 13	2 35
Kilgetty	1 15	2 13	12 36	12 40			2 59	3 3		C R
Saunderfoot										
Bourrile's Court Siding							3 11 3 13		2 47	3 12
Stop Board										
Tenby				12 59			2 21	3 33		C R
Black Rock Siding				X 1 4			2 31	3 34	3 47 4 1	
Penally							3 40	3 42		C R
Lydstep Halt							3 46		X 3 52	4 20
Beavers Hill Halt								3 54		
Lamphey				1 18	1 29					4 30
Pembroke Loop	12 55	1 7 0								
Pembroke			1 22	1 26			3 55		3 59	4 50
Golden Hill Platform										
Pembroke Dock	1 7			1 27						

PEMBROKE DOCK — Up Trains.

STATIONS.	13 Goods. A		14	15 Cattle. F		16 Swansea Passenger. B		17 Cattle and Goods. Z		18 Carmarthen Cattle. C Y	
	arr.	dep.		arr.	dep.	arr.	dep.	arr.	dep.	arr.	dep.
	P.M.	P.M.		A.M.	P.M.	A.M.	P.M.	P.M.	P.M.	P.M.	P.M.
Pembroke Dock	1 15	1 15					2 4		12 1		11
Golden Hill Platform		P 1 24				2 10	2 12	12 17 7 12 49		10.55	
Pembroke	2 45	4 20				2 14	2 17				
Pembroke Loop								3 54			
Lamphey						3 21		X 4 2			
Beavers Hill Halt									1 6		
Lydstep Halt						2 39			1 10		C R
Penally						2 37		2 37			
Black Rock Siding											
Tenby						2 35		3 30	1 56	1 15	
Bourrile's Court Siding											
Saunderfoot				10 10	3 25	2 57 X 3 1		3 5		3 32	
Kilgetty	1 15 12			3 25			3 12	3 5 3 12		P 3 28	2 30
Templeton	P 2 21							3 21		3 57	
Stop Board	2 25							3 31 3 46		4 15	
Narberth	2 43	4 27				2 50	3 30				
Whitland											

U To terminate at Templeton unless there is Up Line Traffic at Kilgetty.
J S.T. 29 and 246.

L From Saunderfoot if required to convey Up Line Traffic from Kilgetty.
X Runs last Monday in each month.
S.T. Nos. 631, 632, 634, 635 Mondays, Wednesdays and Fridays.

Working Timetables for Summer 1935

WHITLAND AND PEMBROKE DOCK.

Single Line worked by Electric Train Staff.

Sections.	Crossing Stations.	Sections.	Crossing Stations.
Whitland and Narberth	Whitland	Tenby and Manorbier	Tenby
Narberth and Templeton	Narberth	Manorbier and Pembroke	Manorbier
Templeton & Saundersfoot	Templeton	Pembroke & Pembroke Dock	Pembroke & Pembroke Dock
Saundersfoot and Tenby	Saundersfoot		

Assistant Engines on Tenby Branch Trains.

Engines assisting Down Passenger or Goods Trains are to be taken off at Templeton, where the Trains are to stop specially for the purpose. Engines assisting Up Branch Passenger Trains are to be taken off at Narberth. Engines assisting Up Branch Goods Trains may be detached at Narberth or Whitland as may be most convenient.

DOWN TRAINS. WEEK DAYS.

Mile Post Mileage.		Distance from Whitland.		STATIONS.	Station No.	K Goods.		B Passenger.		C Parcels. RR	K Goods.	
						arr.	dep.	arr.	dep.	dep.	arr.	dep.
M.	C.	M.	C.			A.M.	A.M.	A.M.	A.M.	A.M.	A.M.	A.M.
258	74	—	—	**Whitland**	3609	—	4 55	—	5 35	Z	—	7 45
264	8	5	14	Narberth	3759	5 10	5 25	5 45	5 47	....	8 0	X 9 17
266	0	7	6	Stop Board	—	P	5 35	—	—	..	—	P9 27
267	14	8	20	Templeton	3760	5 43	● 6 15	—	5 56	7 30	9 35	X10 10
269	62	10	68	Kilgetty	3761	6 23	6 50	—	6 2	7 50	10 18	10 35
270	40	11	46	Saundersfoot	3762	6 55	7 5	6 4	6 6	7 52	10 40	10 45
270	75	12	1	Bonville's Court Siding	3763	7 10	7 25	—	—	—		
273	71	14	77	Stop Board	—	P	7 30	—	—	—	P	10 55
274	53	15	59	**Tenby**	3764	7 35	X 8 55	6 14	6 18	8 0	11 0	X11 40
275	16	16	22	Black Rock Siding	3766	—	—	—	—	—		
275	71	16	77	Penally	3767	When		—	6 22	..	CR	
277	41	18	47	Lydstep Halt	3768	utilised to		—	—	—		
279	9	20	15	Manorbier	3769	work 7.30		—	6 30	..	11 53	X12 5
269	75	21	1	Beavers Hill Halt	3770	a.m. Parcels		—	—	....		
282	49	23	55	Lamphey	3771	Templeton		—	6 36	..	CR	
283	75	25	1	Pembroke Loop	3772	to Tenby,		—	—	....		
284	10	25	16	Pembroke	3772	**Goods** runs		6 39	6 41	..	12 25	12 30
284	58	25	64	Golden Hill Platform	3773	later from		—	—	..		
286	22	27	28	**Pembroke Dock**	3775	Saundersfoot.	6 47	—	—	..	12 40	X —

PEMBROKE DOCK TO WHITLAND.

UP TRAINS. WEEK DAYS.

Distance from Pembroke Dock.		STATIONS.	A Paddington Passenger.		K Goods.		B Passenger		K Cattle and Goods. SX		K Cattle and Goods. SO	
			arr.	dep.	arr.	dep.	arr.	dep.	arr.	dep.	arr.	dep.
M.	C.		A.M.	A.M.	A.M.	A.M.	A.M.	A.M.	A.M.	A.M.	A.M.	A.M.
—	—	**Pembroke Dock**	—	—	—	8 0	..	..	—	9 0	—	9 0
1	44	Golden Hill Platform	—	—	...	..	....	....				
2	12	Pembroke	—	—	—	8 6	..	..	9 10	X 9 48	9 10	X 9 48
2	27	Pembroke Loop	—	—	....	....	....	....				
3	53	Lamphey	—	—	—	8 10	..	..	CR		CR	
6	27	Beavers Hill Halt	—	—	...	..	....	....				
7	13	Manorbier	—	—	—	8 18	..	..	10 3	10 10	10 3	10 10
8	61	Lydstep Halt	—	—	....	....	....	....				
10	31	Penally	8 23	8 25	—	—	..	..	CR		CR	
11	6	Black Rock Siding	—	—	....	....	....	....				
11	49	**Tenby**	8 28	8 34	7 35	X 8 55	9 33	9 45	10 25	X11 40	10 25	X11 40
15	27	Bonville's Court Siding	—	—	—	—	—	—	CR		CR	
15	62	Saundersfoot	8 44	X 8 46	9 10	9 28	—	9 56	11 55		11 55	
16	40	Kilgetty	—	8 50	CR		—	10 0	CR		CR	
19	8	Templeton	—	8 57	9 43	●10 20	—	X10 7	12 10	12 15	12 10	●12 45
20	32½	Stop Board	—	—	P	10 30	—	—	P	12 25	P	12 55
22	14	Narberth	—	X 9 6	10 38	X11 15	—	10 16	12 33	12 38	1 3	1 10
27	28	**Whitland**	9 15	9 22	11 30	—	10 25	—	12 53	—	1 25	—

N July 20th to September 14th, inclusive.
Z Worked by engine, van and guard of 4.55 a.m. Whitland Goods.

WHITLAND TO PEMBROKE DOCK.

DOWN TRAINS. — **WEEK DAYS.**

STATIONS	B Passenger arr	dep	B Passenger arr	dep	B Passenger arr	dep	B Passenger arr	dep	K Goods SX arr	dep	A 11.25 a.m. Cardiff Passenger SO arr	dep
	A.M.	A.M.	A.M.	A.M.	A.M.	A.M.	P.M.	P.M.	P.M.	P.M.	P.M. Z	P.M.
Whitland	—	8 10	—	8 50	—	10 40	—	..	—	12 55	1 54	1 59
Narberth	—	8 21	9 0	X9 5	10 50	X10 52	....	....	1 10	1 25	—	2 0
Stop Board	—	—					..	..	—	P1 35	—	—
Templeton	—	8 30	—	9 13	11 0	11 2	....	....	1 43	1 48	—	2 15
Kilgetty	—	8 36	—	9 21	—	11 8	..	..	1 55	1 59	—	2 22
Saundersfoot	8 40	X8 45	9 23	X9 25	11 10	X11 12	..	..	2 4	2 9	2 26	2 32
Bonville's Court Siding	—	—					....	....			—	—
Stop Board	—	—					....	....	—	P2 19	—	—
Tenby	8 53	X8 55	9 33	9 45	11 20	X11 23	1 33	1 50	2 24	X2 40	2 36	X2 39
Black Rock Siding	—	—			—	11 27	—	1 54	2 50	2 54	—	2 47
Penally	—	8 59	..	..	—	11 31	—	1 58	—	—	—	—
Lydstep Halt	—	9 3	....	....	—	11 37	X 2 2				—	2 51
Manorbier	—	9 9	..	..	—	11 37	2 6		3 4	3 35	—	—
Beavers Hill Halt	—	9 11	..	..	—	11 43	2 10		C R		—	—
Lamphey	—	9 17	..	..	—	11 43	2 12	X 2 14			—	2 57
Pembroke Loop	—	—	....	....	11 45	11 47	—	2 16	3 50	4 20	3 0	—
Pembroke	9 20	X9 21	9 20	X9 21	11 45	11 47	—	2 16			3 0	—
Golden Hill Platform ..	—	9 24	—	9 24							3 7	—
Pembroke Dock ..	9 28	—	..	—	11 52	—	2 21	—	4 30	—	3 7	—

PEMBROKE DOCK TO WHITLAND.

UP TRAINS. — **WEEK DAYS.**

STATIONS	A Paddington Passenger SO arr	dep	B Passenger arr	dep	A Birmingham Passenger SO arr	dep	B Passenger arr	dep	K Cattle and Goods SX arr	dep	B Pontypool Road Passenger arr	dep
	N A.M.	A.M.	V A.M.	A.M.	Y A.M.	A.M.	P.M.	P.M.	P.M.	P.M.	P.M.	P.M.
Pembroke Dock ..	—	10 20	—	10 50	—	11 35	—	1 0	—	X 12 40	—	2 5
Golden Hill Platform..							—	1 5				
Pembroke	10 25	10 27	10 55	10 57	11 40	11 42	—	1 8	12 50	1 20	2 10	2 12
Pembroke Loop	—	10 31	—	11 1	11 45	X11 45			C R		—	2 16
Lamphey	—	10 31	—	11 1		11 48	—	1 12				
Beavers Hill Halt	—	—	—	—	—	—	—	1 17				
Manorbier	10 38	10 40	11 8	11 9	11 55	X11 56	—	1 20	1 35	X 2 4	2 21	2 22
Lydstep Halt	—	10 44	—	11 13			—	1 24				2 33
Penally	10 48	10 50	11 17	11 19		12 2	1 28	1 30	C R			
Black Rock Siding	—	—										
Tenby	10 53	X11 1	11 22	X11 27	12 5	12 13	1 33	1 50	2 19	X 3 15	2 36	X2 39
Bonville's Court Siding											2 49	2 51
Saundersfoot	11 11	X11 15	11 37	11 39	12 23	12 25	..	..	3 30	3 35	—	2 55
Kilgetty	—	11 17	11 49	11 50			....	....	C R		3 1	3 3
Templeton	—	11 24	—	—			....	....	3 50	3 58	—	—
Stop Board	—	—	—	—			....	....	—	P4 6	3 11	3 15
Narberth	—	11 33	—	11 59	12 41	12 43	....	....	4 13	4 30	3 22	3 32
Whitland	11 42	11 52	12 8	—	12 52	12 57	....	....	4 45	—		

V Will not run on Saturdays, July 20th to September 14th, inclusive.
Y Will not run after September 14th. **Z** July 27th to September 7th, inclusive.

WHITLAND TO PEMBROKE DOCK.

DOWN TRAINS.	WEEK DAYS.											
	A		**A**		**B**		**B**		**B**		**B**	
STATIONS.	8.55 a.m. Paddington Passenger.		9.45 a.m. Birmingham Passenger. SO		Passenger.		Passenger. SX		Passenger.		Passenger.	
	arr.	dep.	arr.	dep.	arr.	dep.	arr.	dep.	arr.	dep.	arr.	dep.
				Y		Z						
	P.M.	P M.	P.M.	P.M.	P.M.	P.M.	P.M.	P.M.	P.M.	P.M	P.M.	P.M.
Whitland	2 14	2 19	4 8	4 13	..	..	..	..	—	5 30	—	7 55
Narberth	—	2 30	—	4 24	....	....	....	....	—	5 41	8 5	8 7
Stop Board	—	—	—	—	..	..	SUS-		—	—	—	—
Templeton	—	2 39	—	4 32	....	....	PENDED		—	5 50	—	8 16
Kilgetty	—	2 45	—	—	....	....	....	....	—	5 56	—	8 22
Saundersfoot	2 47	X 2 50	4 40	X 4 43	....	....	....	....	5 58	X 6 0	8 24	8 26
Bonville's Court Siding	—	—	—	—	....	....	....	....	—	—	—	—
Stop Board	—	—	—	—	....	....	....	....	—	—	—	—
Tenby	2 58	X 3 1	4 51	4 53	—	5 50	5 55	6 5	6 8	6 11	8 34	X 8 38
Black Rock Siding	—	—	—	—	—	—	....	....	—	—	—	—
Penally	—	3 5	—	4 57	—	5 53	—	6 9	—	6 15	8 41	8 43
Lydstep Halt	—	—	—	—	—	5 58	—	6 13	—	6 19	—	8 47
Manorbier	—	3 13	—	5 5	—	6 4	6 18	X 6 21	—	6 25	—	8 53
Beavers Hill Halt	—	—	—	—	—	6 6	—	6 23	—	—	—	—
Lamphey	—	3 19	—	—	—	6 10	—	6 28	—	6 31	—	9 0
Pembroke Loop	—	—	—	5 X 13	—	—	—	—	6 33	X 6 35	—	—
Pembroke	3 22	3 24	5 14	5 16	—	6 14	—	6 32	6 36	6 38	—	9 4
Golden Hill Platform	—	—	—	—	—	6 17	—	6 35	—	—	—	—
Pembroke Dock	3 30	—	5 21	—	6 21	—	6 39	8 0	6 43	—	9 9	—

PEMBROKE DOCK TO WHITLAND.

UP TRAINS.	WEEK DAYS.										
	B		**B**				**B**		**B**		**B**
STATIONS.	Passenger.		Passenger. SO				Passenger.		Passenger. SO		Passenger.
	arr.	dep.	arr.	dep.			arr.	dep.	arr.	dep.	arr.	dep.
	P.M.	P.M.	P.M.	P.M.			P.M.	P.M.	P.M.	P.M.	P.M.	P.M.
Pembroke Dock	—	4 0	—	5 0	..	..	—	5 5	..	..	—	6 25
Golden Hill Platform	—	—	—	5 3	....	....	—	5 10	....	....		
Pembroke	—	X 4 6	—	5 8	....	....	—	5 13	N		6 32	6 34
Pembroke Loop	—	—	5 9	X 5 11	....	....	—	—	....	....		X
Lamphey	—	4 10	—	5 18	....	....	—	5 18	..	..	—	6 38
Beavers Hill Halt	—	4 15	—	5 24	....	....	—	5 24	..	..		
Manorbier	—	4 18	—	5 28	....	....	—	5 28	..	..	6 45	6 47
Lydstep Halt	—	4 22	—	5 32	....	....	—	5 32	....	....		
Penally	—	4 27	—	5 37	..	..	—	5 37	..	..	6 52	6 54
Black Rock Siding	—	—	—	—	....	....	—	—	....	....		
Tenby	4 30	4 32	5 40	—	..	..	5 40	—	—	5 45	6 57	7 0
Bonville's Court Siding	—	—	—	—	..	..	—	—	....	....		
Saundersfoot	4 42	X 4 43			..	..			5 55	X 5 59	7 10	7 12
Kilgetty	—	4 47			....	....			—	6 3	—	7 16
Templeton	—	4 54			....	....			—	6 10	—	7 23
Stop Board	—	—			....	....			—	—		
Narberth	5 2	5 3			....	....			—	6 19	7 31	7 33
Whitland	5 12	—			....	....			6 28	—	7 42	—

(centre columns: "July 13th to Sept. 14th, inclusive." and "Sats. excepted July 13th to Sept. 14th, inclusive.")

N—July 27th to Sept. 7th, inclusive. Y—Will not run after Sept. 14th.

Z—Will not run on Saturdays, July 27th to Sept. 7th, inclusive.

WHITLAND TO PEMBROKE DOCK.

DOWN TRAINS.	WEEK DAYS.	SUNDAYS.				
	B	A	B	A	B	B
STATIONS.	Passenger. WSO	10.25 p.m. Paddington Passenger. Z	Passenger. V	10.30 a.m. Birmingham Passenger. Z	Passenger. Z	Passenger.
	arr. dep.	arr. dep.	arr. dep.	arr. dep.	arr. dep.	arr. dep.
	P.M. P.M.	A.M. A.M	P.M. P.M.	P.M. P.M.	P.M. P.M.	P.M. P.M.
Whitland	.. ..	4 50 4 55	.. ..	4 28 4 30	— 7 35	.. ..
Narberth	....	— 5 0	....	— 4 44	7 45 7 47	....
Stop Board	.. ..	— 5 15	.. ..	— 4 55	7 55 7 57	.. ..
Templeton	....	— 5 15	....	— 4 55	7 55 7 57	....
Kilgetty	.. ..	— 5 21	.. ..	—	— 8 3	....
Saundersfoot	....	5 25 5 27	.. ..	5 0 5 2	8 5 8 7	....
Bonville's Court Siding	.. ..	— —	.. ..	— —	— —	.. ..
Stop Board	....	5 36 5 38	.. ..	— —	— —	.. ....
Tenby	10 29 11 0	5 36 5 38	3 1 3 10	5 11 5 15	8 15 8 30	9 45 10 10
Black Rock Siding	11 3 11 5	— 5 42	— 3 14	—	— 8 34	— 10 14
Penally	— —	—	— 3 18	—	— 8 38	— —
Lydstep Halt	— —	— 5 50	— 3 24	— 5 22	8 43 8 45	10 21 10 23
Manorbier	— 11 15	— 5 50	— 3 24	— 5 22	8 43 8 45	10 21 10 23
Beavers Hill Halt ..	— —	— —	— —	—	— 8 52	— 10 30
Lamphey	— 11 19	— 5 56	— 3 31	—	— —	— —
Pembroke Loop	— —	— —	— —	—	— 8 56	10 33 10 35
Pembroke	— 11 25	— 6 1	3 31 3 35	— 5 35	— 8 56	10 33 10 35
Golden Hill Platform	— —	— —	— —	—	— —	— —
Pembroke Dock ..	11 29 —	6 6 —	3 40 6 0	5 38 —	9 1 9 15	10 40 —

PEMBROKE DOCK TO WHITLAND.

UP TRAINS.	WEEK DAYS.		SUNDAYS.			
	B	B	A	B	B	B
STATIONS.	Passenger.	Passenger. WSO	Birmingham Passenger. V	Passenger. Z	Passenger. Z	Passenger. Z
	arr. dep	arr. dep.	arr. dep.	arr. dep.	arr. dep.	arr. dep.
	P.M. P.M.	P.M. P.M.	P.M. P.M.	P.M. P.M.	P.M. P.M.	P.M. P.M.
Pembroke Dock	— 8 5	— 10 0	— 12 30	— 2 30	3 40 6 0	9 1 9 15
Golden Hill Platform	— —	— —	— —	— —	— —	— —
Pembroke	— 8 11	— 10 7	12 35 12 36	2 35 2 37	6 5 6 7	9 20 9 22
Pembroke Loop	— —	— —	— —	— —	— —	— —
Lamphey	— 8 15	— 10 11	— —	— 2 41	— 6 11	— 9 26
Beavers Hill Halt ..	FSO 8 20	— —	— —	— —	— —	— —
Manorbier	— 8 23	— 10 19	12 48	— 2 49	— 6 19	— 9 34
Lydstep Halt	— 8 27	— —	— —	— 2 53	— 6 23	— —
Penally	— 8 32	10 24 10 26	— —	— 2 58	6 27 6 29	9 40 9 42
Black Rock Siding ..	— —	— —	— —	— —	— —	— —
Tenby	8 35 8 37	10 29 11 0	12 57 1 1	3 1 3 10	6 32 6 36	9 45 10 10
Bonville's Court Siding	— —	— —	— —	— —	— —	— —
Saundersfoot	— 8 48	....	— 1 12	....	6 46 6 48	.. ....
Kilgetty	— 8 52	.. ..	— 1 18	.. ..	— 6 52	.. ..
Templeton	— 8 59	.... ..	— 1 22	.. ..	— 6 59	.. ..
Stop Board	— —	.. ..	— 1 31	....	7 7 7 9	....
Narberth	— 9 8	.. ..	— 1 31	....	7 7 7 9	....
Whitland	9 17 —	.. ..	1 40 1 45	.. ..	7 18 —	.. ..

V—July 28th to September 1st, inclusive.

Z—Will not run after September 15th.

Maximum Speed of Trains through Junctions and other Specified Places—continued.

Name of Place.	Direction of Train.		Miles per Hour.
	From	To	

WHITLAND AND PEMBROKE DOCK BRANCH.

DOWN TRAINS.

Mixed Trains and Goods Trains between Whitland and Pembroke Dock must not exceed a speed of 25 miles per hour.

Whitland Station	To P. & T. Branch	15
Narberth Station	Any Train through Station ..	15
Narberth and Templeton ..	Between 264m. 15c. and 264m. 40c. ..	25
Templeton Station	Any Train through Station ..	15
Saundersfoot Station	,, ,, ,, ,, ..	15
Saundersfoot and Tenby ..	Between 272m. 60c. and 273m. 60c. ..	25
Tenby Yard	Over Loop Junction at Penally end between 274m. 61c. and 274m. 64c.	15
Manorbier Station	Any Train through Station ..	15
Pembroke Station	Between 284m. 10c. and 284m. 22c. ..	20

UP TRAINS.

Mixed Trains and Goods Trains between Pembroke Dock and Whitland must not exceed a speed of 25 miles per hour.

Pembroke Station	Between 284m. 22c. and 284m. 10c. ..	20
Tenby Yard	Over Loop Junction at Penally end between 274m. 64c. and 274m. 61c.	15
Tenby Station	Any Train through Station ..	15
Tenby and Saundersfoot ..	Between 273m. 60c. and 272m. 60c. ..	25
Templeton and Narberth ..	Between 264m. 40c. and 264m. 15c. ..	25
Narberth Station	Any Train through Station ..	15
Whitland Station	From P & T. Branch	15

LIST OF SIGNAL BOXES—continued.

Distance Box to Box.	Name of Box.	TIMES DURING WHICH BOXES ARE OPEN.					Whether Provided with Switch.
		Week Days.			Sundays.		
		Opened.		Closed at	Opened at	Closed at	
		Mondays.	Other Days.				

WHITLAND AND PEMBROKE DOCK BRANCH.

5 5¾	Narberth	4.50 a.m.	4.50 a.m.		6.50 p.m.**A**		8. 0 p.m.	
3 10¼	Templeton	5.20 a.m.	5.20 a.m.		6.35 p.m.**B**		8.10 p.m.	
3 21¼	Saundersfoot ..	5.45 a.m.	5.45 a.m.		6.15 p.m.**C**		8.20 p.m.	
4 15	Tenby	5.55 a.m.	5.55 a.m.	After last train.	2.45 p.m.**E** / 8. 0 p.m.	Not after September 13th.	6.50 p.m. / 10.25 p.m.	No.
4 33¼	Manorbier	6.10 a.m.	6.10 a.m.		2.30 p.m.**D** / 8.15 p.m.		6.35 p.m. / 10.35 p.m.	
4 74¼	Pembroke	6.20 a.m.	6.20 a.m.		2.25 p.m.**F** / 8.35 p.m.		6.25 p.m. / 10.40 p.m.	
2 5	Pembroke Dock ..	6.30 a.m.	6.30 a.m.		2. 0 p.m.**G** / 8.50 p.m.		6.10 p.m. / 10.55 p.m.	

A—To open from 1.15 p.m. to 2.15 p.m. and 4.30 p.m. to 8. 0 p.m. ⎫
B — ,, ,, ,, 1. 5 p.m. to 2. 5 p.m. and 4.40 p.m. to 8.10 p.m. ⎬ July 28th to September 1st, inclusive.
C — ,, ,, ,, 12.55 p.m. to 1.55 p.m. and 4.50 p.m. to 8.20 p.m. ⎭
D—To also open at 12.30 p.m. ⎫
E — ,, ,, ,, ,, 12.40 p.m. ⎬ July 28th to September 1st, inclusive.
F — ,, ,, ,, ,, 12.25 p.m. ⎪
G — ,, ,, ,, ,, 12. 0 noon ⎭
T—After clearing of 8.25 p.m. Paddington to Neyland Parcels Train.
V—July 28th to September 1st inclusive.

During the time the Signal Boxes are closed no Train or Engine must call at either of the Stations unless it is timed, or unless special arrangements have been made for it to do so. The fixed signals will only be used for any Train or Engine calling at the Stations named during the time they are switched in.

When it is possible for any of the Signal Boxes to close on Sunday mornings earlier than the times shewn above this must be done, and the signalmen should keep in touch with the Control Office as to the movement of the trains.

STANDARD LOADS OF PASSENGER, ETC., TRAINS—continued.

From	To	4001-4072 except 4009, 4016, 4082, 4087, "Halls" 49 & 59XX	99XX except 43, 53, 63, 73, 83 & 93XX, 31, 41, 51 & 61XX, 56 & 96XX	Bull Dog 33XX, 34XX	4400-4410, 4500-4599, 5500-5574, 56, 57, 67, 87 & 97XX	0-6-0 and 0-6-0 T. "A" Group
WHITLAND and PEMBROKE DOCK.		Tons.	Tons.	Tons.	Tons.	Tons.
Whitland ...	Templeton ...	288†	252	182	192	160
Templeton ...	Pembroke Dock ...	300	288	216X	224X	192X
Pembroke Dock ...	Tenby ...	300	288	216	224	216
Tenby ...	Narberth ...	288†	252	182	192	160
Narberth...	Whitland ...	300	288	250	250	250

† —"Halls" 20 tons less between Whitland and Templeton and Tenby and Narberth.

X —Load 10 tons less for trains calling at Golden Hill Halt.

MAXIMUM LOADS FOR BRANCH FREIGHT TRAINS—continued.

MAXIMUM ENGINE LOADS.

SECTION. From	To	WORKING LOADS. Maximum number of wagons to be conveyed except for Trains specially provided for in the Service Book or by arrangement.	Group A — Traffic Class 1	Class 2	Class 3	Empties	Group B — Traffic Class 1	Class 2	Class 3	Empties	Group C — Traffic Class 1	Class 2	Class 3	Empties	Group D — Traffic Class 1	Class 2	Class 3	Empties	Group E — Traffic Class 1	Class 2	Class 3	Empties
Pembroke Dock.																						
Whitland ...	Templeton	22	12	14	18	24	14	17	21	28	15	18	23	30	20	24	30	40	24	29	36	48
Templeton ...	Tenby ...	35	24	29	36	48	28	34	42	56	30	36	45	60	40	48	60	80	48	58	73	96
Tenby ...	Pembroke ...	24	18	22	27	36	21	25	32	42	22	26	33	44	30	36	45	60	36	43	54	72
Pembroke ...	Pembroke Dock..	24	13	16	20	26	15	18	23	30	16	19	24	31	21	25	32	42	26	31	39	52
Pembroke Dock ...	Pembroke ...	24	18	22	27	36	21	25	33	44	22	26	33	44	30	36	45	60	36	43	54	72
Pembroke ...	Tenby ...	24	19	23	29	38	22	26	33	44	24	29	36	48	31	37	47	63	38	46	57	76
Tenby ...	Narberth ...	22	10	12	15	20	11	13	17	22	12	14	18	24	16	19	24	32	20	24	30	40
Narberth ...	Whitland ...	50	25	30	36	50	29	35	44	58	31	37	47	62	41	49	62	82	50	60	75	100

* Fine weather load.   † Bad weather load.   ‡ To include any proportion of 12-ton vehicles.

X May include 20 twelve-ton empties, all other twelve-tonners to be calculated as five twelve-tonners equal six-ten tonners.   Z The Maximum Load of a Freight Train worked by two engines of any type between Garnant and Pantyffynnon must not exceed the length of 70 ten or twelve ton loaded wagons or equivalent in weight thereto.

Appendix Two: List of Passenger Stock

Pembroke & Tenby Railway

DESCRIPTIVE LIST OF ——— GAUGE PASSENGER STOCK.

July 9th 1896

Appendix Three: List of Locomotive Engines

DESCRIPTIVE LIST OF 4'8½" GAUGE LOCOMOTIVE ENGINES.

Pembroke and Tenby Railway.

July 1896.

No. of Engine		DATE of BUILD		MAKER	Original Cost (including Tender) £	Tender or Tank	Weight in Working order	CYLINDERS			WHEELS					WHEEL BASE L. to T.	BOILER BARREL		FIREBOX		TUBES			Working PRESSURE		MILEAGE from date of Starting or date of Renewal to	TANK Capacity in Gallons	Engine stationed at	If in working order or under repair	Value 1896 £	REMARKS
Plate	Constr.	Starting	re-built					Inch Dia.	No.	Stroke	Total No.	No. Coupled	Dia. Lead	Driving	Trail.	Descrip. Kind of Tyre Flanging		Length	Out side dia.	Length inside made.	Out side dia.	No.	Length	per square inch	Date						
2		1863	1890	Sharp, Stewart & Co		Tank	25 10	13	14		6	Single	6 3 6 3 0 3 6			12 8	9 6 3 8	3 8 3 0	2	Iron 1 36	140 lbs		450	Tenby	Working order	600	
3		1866	1887	Do		Tender	26	16 20		6	3 6 3 6 3 6				14	3 9 10 3	11 4 3	8	136 10 3	2 Brass 1887	140			Whitland		900	
4		1865	1889	Do		do	27 10	16 24		6	4 6 4 6 4 6				11	4 9 10 4	0 4 11 4	9	136 10 2	2 Iron 1896	140			Pembroke Dock		1,000	New narrow gauge Passenger Pass
5		1867	1893	Do		do	31	16 24		6	4 6 4 6 4 6				14	9 9 10 4	3 5 11 4	9	172 10 3	2 Brass 1893	140			Tenby	Under Renews	1,400	
6		1872	1895	Do		do	31	16 24		6	4 6 4 6 4 6				11	9 9 10 4	3 5 11 4	9	172 10 3	2 Iron 1895	140				Working order	1,000	Brown goods now sold to Tenby. No. old Passenger & Mineral Brown
7		1882		G.W.R. Co	2000	Tank	43	17 24		6	4 6 4 6 4 6				15	6 10 4	4 5 14 4	9	218 10 8	11 1891	140		1150	Pembroke Dock		1,000	
8		1895		Do	3200	Tender	36	17 26		6	3 6 5 0 5				16	112 10 4	6 5 14 4	9	218 10 9	11 1895	140			Tenby		1,200	
		C																										£ 7,100	

GREAT WESTERN RAILWAY.   LOCOMOTIVE DEPARTMENT.

Particulars of Shed and other accommodation for Running Engines at _Tenby_ Station.

ENGINE SHED (Sketch Plan to be attached).	Large Shed	Small Shed
How built (Stone, Brick or Wood)	Wood	Wood
Length	56.0	28.0
Breadth	20.0	14.0
Height to top of roof ridge	19.0	19.0
Do. do. wall plate	13.6	14.0
Cubical contents	18.200 c.ft	6.666
Style of Roof (Gable, Hip Gable or Saw-tooth)	Gable	Gable
Roof principals (Material)	Wood (Felted)	Wood (Slates)
If fitted with Smoke Troughs	Yes (one)	No
Date built, or date Shed was first used	1863	1863
Length of each Line used for running Engines	one — 56.0	one — 28.0
Do. do. do. repairs	—	—
Engine Pits—Length of each used for running Engines	53.0	27.0
Do. do. do. repairs	—	—

OUTSIDE SHED

Lines available for standing Engines	See facing
Engine Pits—length of each	"
Do. at Station	"

ENGINE TURNTABLES

Diameter	one	18.6
Length of Rail		18.4
Girders (Material)		Iron
How turned		Pushed round by projecting lever
Where fixed		Between Large & Small Shed
Date fixed		1863
Maker		Astbury - Manchester.

COAL STAGE.

Sketch and size	—
Number of Crates or Tips	Crane No. N 131.
How built (Stone Brick or Wood)	Stone & Brick 1863
Date built	1863

SAND FURNACE — Nil —

Outside dimensions	length, breadth, height,
Brief description and Sketch	
Date built	
When started	

SHOPS OR OFFICES OUTSIDE THE SHED	Loco Fitting Shop	Wagon Shop	Boiler Engine & Machine Shop	Smith Shop	Old Foundry & Store	Old Slate Store
How built (Stone, Brick or Wood)	Wood	Stone & Wood	Stone & Wood	Stone	Stone	Stone
Length	64.0 / 40.0	14.0	See facing	29.0	35.0	
Breadth	43.0 / 28.0	40.0	24.0	15.6		
Height to top of roof ridge	30.0	27.6	23.0	19.0		
Do. do. wall plate	17.0	15.6	11.0	12.0		
Cubical contents	86.570	63.960	26.090	11.832	8.780	
Style of Roof (Gable, Hip Gable or Saw-tooth)	Gable	Gable	Gable to Gable	Gable	Gable	
Roof principals (Material)	Wood (Slates)	Wood (Slates)	Wood (Slates)	Wood (Slates)	Wood (Slates)	
Date built, or date opened						
Length of Line used for repairs	105.0 / 64.0	42.0 / 42.0				
Do. Engine Pit used for repairs	85.0 / 45.0	30.0				

Inside dimensions

Superintendent's Signature.